PLACES TO GO WITH
CHILDREN IN
WASHINGTON D.C.

PLACES TO GO WITH CHILDREN IN
WASHINGTON D.C.

Judy Colbert

Chronicle Books • San Francisco

Printed in the United States of America.

Library of Congress Cataloging in Publication Data
Colbert, Judy.
    Places to go with children in Washington, D.C. / Judy Colbert.
        p.   cm.
    Includes index.
    ISBN 0-87701-818-9
    1. Washington (D.C.)—Description—1981–   —Guide-books.
    2. Family recreation—Washington (D.C.)—Guide-books.
    3. Children—Travel—Washington (D.C.)—Guide-books.
        I. Title
    F192.3.C64   1991   90-27630
    917.5304'4—dc20   CIP

Book design and composition: Words & Deeds
Cover design: Karen Smidth
Map courtesy Washington Metropolitan Area Transit Authority

Distributed in Canada by Raincoast Books,
112 East Third Avenue, Vancouver, B.C. V5T 1C8

10 9 8 7 6 5 4 3 2 1

Chronicle Books
275 Fifth Street
San Francisco, CA 94103

♻ printed on recycled paper

Dedicated, with love and joy, to Arlene and Jazzlyn.

Contents

Introduction

Welcome to sightseeing in Washington, D.C. You will join some 20 million people who come to discover the beauty and history of this area every year.

Places to Go with Children in and around Washington, D.C. will help you select those sights that widen the eyes, quicken the pulse, stimulate the senses, inspire the imagination, stir the heart, bring goosebumps to the fore, fire up patriotism, and gladden the soul. Everything is here, from curiosities of the medieval world to state-of-tomorrow scientific wonders.

Emphasis is placed on that which is interesting to specific age groups, from preschool to high school, and, shh, what's educational about them. A dollhouse collection is a dollhouse collection, but it's also a lesson in architecture. Little detail is provided on the history of a building, unless the description will add something to the experience before you arrive at the sight. If you and the children learn something, how serendipitous. I love to see noses pressed up against the display case, eyes wide in amazement, and a passion growing to find out more about something, whether it's science, history, art, or geography.

Places also provides answers to some of the tricky little questions children expect you to know. Why are those columns in the middle of the arboretum? Why can you hear whispers in Statuary Hall at the Capitol? If I can see the top of the Washington Monument from the gallery at the Washington National Cathedral, is the cathedral taller than the monument?

As one local bank advertises, this is the most important city in the world. It may be, but it also is a living city, populated by normal people going about their everyday lives.

What differentiates you from them is your perspective and the city's design. The layout may perplex you at first, but you will soon realize that the city's large and small parks were designed to keep the confusion away from you. Look at the Mall with its wall of museums and galleries and rows of trees that keep Washington, the city, outside the perimeters of Washington, the tourist attraction. These barriers create a quiet sanctuary from the city's noise and protect you from the bustle of the outside world. All is tranquil within these borders, at least once you've found a parking place. (You'll be wise to use public transportation, such as the subway system, as much as possible.) The same serenity can be found in Rock Creek Park, the National Arboretum, Kenilworth Aquatic Gardens, and the many regional parks in Virginia and Maryland.

There is so much to see and do, and our energy, attention span, and time are so finite, that it's important to have your own design of what you want to do. Create your own barrier: Inside that wall include what you and the children want to do. Outside that wall is confusion and the intrusion of things that are fascinating, but not high on your priority list.

Let the children help make the plans. Don't plan too many activities. Lines will be longer than you expected. You'll want to spend more time than you programmed at some place. It will rain the day you schedule the zoo visit. It will be hotter, or you'll have to walk farther than you anticipated. A carefully detailed, hourly agendum will be down the tubes. Besides that, tempers will flare, and your trip memories will not be pleasant. Be flexible. If you end up with an extra half day, use that time to relax in one of the parks, or have a standby place to visit.

An ideal sightseeing trip considers the geographical location of the places to be visited. Save energy by seeing all of the buildings along Capitol Hill together, then the buildings on the Mall together, in sequence. Don't go from the Library of Congress to the National Zoo, back to the National Air and Space Museum, to Arlington National Cemetery, and then to the National Cathedral. You'll spend too much time in transportation.

There is no paragon trip. If you want to play with the tarantulas at the Museum of Natural History or watch the sharks being fed at the National Aquarium, you have to bend to their schedule, even if the perfect plan says you should be at the National Archives at that moment. And, if you want to save two hours of waiting time, you have to be at the Bureau of Printing and Engraving the first thing in the morning. The secret is good planning to avoid disappointment and not to pack too much into any one day.

My touring philosophy comes from years of sightseeing with children and my first visit to France. I have two very vivid memories of that trip. The first is of the tour guide pushing, pushing, pushing, telling us we were in France for only a short time and had much to see, for who knew when we would return. Also, the guide said we would not remember our fatigue. Baloney. I may not feel the exhaustion any more, but I remember it. I do not recall much of what we saw because things started blurring together.

The second distinct mental keepsake is of schoolchildren sitting at the feet of a docent in the Hall of Mirrors in the Palace at Versailles. They were learning about their history, in French, of course, and I thought how wonderful and amazing that they can do this (speak French at that age and be able to visit this historic place in their backyard, a place that people come to see from all over the world). It then occurred to me that everyone who visits Washington has that same experience. How basic, but how astounding!

Our bank advertising may overstate the case to say Washington is the most important city in the world, but it certainly is one of the most beautiful, most exciting, and most interesting. Enjoy yourself!

Before You Visit

Now, let's get to the nitty-gritty. First, you should write to the tourism bureau for the area you will be visiting. The respective addresses and phone numbers are at the end of this section. These offices can provide information about hotels, restaurants, shopping, special events, and other timely information.

If you want a VIP tour of the White House, passes into the House or Senate galleries, foreign policy briefings in the Department of State, the FBI tour, or if you want to buy a flag flown over the Capitol (which will include a letter from the architect of the Capitol with the date the flag was flown over the building), then write to your congressional representative at the specific office building, if you know it. (The House of Representatives ZIP code is 20515, the Senate ZIP code is 20510.) Call the congressional switchboard at (202) 224-3121 for address and telephone information.

You should write at least one month in advance (six months is not too early for some passes), and state when you'll be visiting, how many in your party, and what you want to do. Once you arrive, visit your representative and sign the guest book. If there's time, you may be able to have your photo taken with your representative or senator on the Capitol steps.

Once you're in town, stop by the Washington Visitor Information Center (the address is at the end of this section) to pick up additional free brochures, maps, and advice. Many of these materials are available in foreign languages. The International Visitors Information Service is at 733 15th Street, NW, Suite 300, Washington, D.C. 20005. Call (202) 783-6540 for more extensive foreign language brochures about Washington.

There are several "Dial" numbers that will give you current information on a variety of subjects. Among the most popular are: Dial-An-Event (202) 737-8866 for a recording of major events, Dial-A-Hike (202) 547-2326, Dial-A-Park (202) 485-PARK for National Park Service schedules, Dial-A-Museum (202) 357-2020 for Smithsonian Institution activities, and Dial-A-Phenomenon (202) 737-8855 for announcements on the planets, stars, and worldwide occurences.

There are three telephone exchanges in the Washington area: (202) for Washington, (703) for suburban Virginia, and (301) for suburban Maryland. To call from suburban Maryland into Washington or Virginia, you need to use the area code, but you do not need to precede it with 1. These are toll-free numbers within the Washington suburban area. Other calls, such as from Washington to Baltimore, or from Maryland to some Virginia locations, will need the 1 and there will be a toll charge. A new area code, 410, is being introduced in Maryland in late 1991.

Study a map of the area you will be visiting. Washington is divided into four sections, Northwest (NW), Northeast (NE), Southeast (SE), and Southwest (SW), of which the Northwest section is the largest. The dividing lines set out from the Capitol, so north of East Capitol Street is Northeast, and south of it is Southeast. Streets running north and south are numbered, starting at the Capitol. Those running east and west are lettered and run alphabetically with a single letter (I Street often is spelled out Eye Street, and there isn't a J street in the northwest quadrant) and then two syllable words, followed by three syllable words, and so on. Irving Street will be in the second alphabet, Brandywine in the third. The diagonal roadways are avenues and are named for states. They create the circles and the most confusion for visitors.

Many of the museums and galleries in the Washington area are open all year, except Christmas Day. Some also are closed on Thanksgiving and New Year's days. Others are closed on major holidays, or as they're generally known in this area, federal holidays. These are Martin Luther King Day, Washington's Birthday, Memorial Day, Fourth of July, Labor Day, Columbus Day, and Veterans Day. The listings will note if a place is closed on these holidays.

Metrorail and Metrobus are the easiest ways to travel. Most major museums and many galleries are within easy walking distance from Metrorail stops, eliminating the need to look for a parking place, feed the meter, and make sure you're out of the space by rush hour. Additionally, after a day of sightseeing and walking, it's nice to be able to relax on the subway before tackling the roads.

For detailed, door-to-door instructions on which bus or subway to take and at what time, call the Metro office at (202) 637-7000 daily between 6 A.M. and 11:30 P.M. Subway lines are referred to by their colors (red, blue, orange, yellow, green) or destinations. For example, the orange line goes to New Carrollton (Maryland) and Vienna (Virginia). You can transfer from one line to another without extra

M metro

Shady Grove

MARC Rockville

Twinbrook

White Flint

Grosvenor

Medical Center

Bethesda

Friendship Heights

RED LINE

Tenleytown-AU

Van Ness-UDC

Cleveland Park

Woodley Park-Zoo

Dupont Circle

Farragut North

McPherson Sq

Wheaton

Forest Glen

Silver Spring **MARC**

Takoma

Fort Totten

Brookland-CUA

Rhode Island Ave

MARC New Carrollton

Landover

Cheverly

Deanwood

Minnesota Ave

Union Station **MARC**

Gallery Pl.-Chinatown

Judiciary Sq

ORANGE LINE

Rosslyn

Vienna

Dunn Loring

West Falls Church

East Falls Church

Ballston

Virginia Sq-GMU

Clarendon

Court House

Arlington Cemetery

Foggy Bottom-GWU

Farragut West

Metro Center

Federal Triangle

Smithsonian

Archives-Navy Mem'l

L'Enfant Plaza

Federal Center SW

Capitol South

Eastern Market

Potomac Ave

Stadium-Armory

Benning Road

Capitol Heights

Addison Road

BLUE LINE

Pentagon

Pentagon City

YELLOW LINE

Crystal City

National Airport

Braddock Rd

King Street

Eisenhower Ave

Huntington

Legend

Red Line — Wheaton/Shady Grove

Blue Line — Addison Road/National Airport

Orange Line — New Carrollton/Vienna

Yellow Line — Gallery Pl-Chinatown/Huntington

◯ Transfer station

All day Parking

MARC Commuter Rail Service

N

charge. See the lobby of each station for specific directions, or write to the Washington Metropolitan Area Transit Authority (WMATA), 600 Fifth Street, NW, Washington, D.C. 20001.

The subway runs from 5:30 A.M. to midnight weekdays, 8 A.M. to midnight Saturday, and 10 A.M. to midnight Sunday. Rush hours are 5:30 to 9:30 A.M. and 3 to 7 P.M., and rates, which are based on distance traveled, are higher during these hours. A third automobile rush hour is developing downtown during the lunch hour, but this is not reflected in the subway fares.

The subway operates with a Farecard, which you can purchase at any station. Children under five, traveling with a parent or other paying passenger, ride free. On weekends and holidays (except the Fourth of July, when the fare is 75 cents), there's a $6 family Farecard that permits a family of four to ride the entire system all Saturday and Sunday. Normal fares range from 85 cents to $2.55, depending on time of day and length of travel. Family Farecards can be purchased at one of the numerous Metro sales offices, or at many hotel concierge desks. Some sites may charge a small fee.

You may transfer for free from the subway to a Metro bus. Pick up the transfer in the subway station you enter on your way home; do not wait to pick up the transfer at your destination station because it is not valid. You cannot use a transfer to change from a bus to the subway.

Every station is accessible by elevator. Floor lights along the tracks flash on and off when a train is entering the station to alert the hearing impaired, and a horn sounds when doors are about to open or close to aid the visually impaired. Wheelchair space is designated on the subway, but remember all space is at a premium during rush hour. Reduced fares are available for handicapped and senior citizens.

Metrorail offers an added bonus: Many children have never been on a train before, so this system can be a good introduction to rail travel.

Once downtown, you can take the Tourmobile or the Old Town Trolley to get from one sightseeing spot to another. In either case you will enjoy a narrated tour and be able to disembark at any stop to shop, sightsee, or eat, and reboard later for no extra charge. Both services run about every 20 or 30 minutes.

The Tourmobile runs from 9 A.M. to 6:30 P.M. June 15 to Labor Day and 9:30 A.M. to 4:30 P.M. the rest of the year. Tickets can be purchased from ticket booths at most of the stops or from the driver. Fares start at $8 for adults and $4 for children from 3 to 11, with higher rates for tickets good for one and one-half days or two days and for optional tours. Call (202) 554-7950 (recording) or (202) 554-7020 for information.

There are 18 stops on the 90-minute (or longer) Tourmobile ride, with options for going through Arlington National Cemetery, Mount Vernon, and the Frederick Douglass home (depending on the season). Reservations are recommended for the latter two sights. Tourmobile stops are the Washington Monument (15th Street, NW), Arts and Industries, National Air and Space Museum, Union Station, United States Capitol (First Street and Independence Avenue, SE), National Gallery of Art, Museum of Natural History, National Museum of American History, Bureau of Engraving and Printing, Jefferson Memorial (and Tidal Basin), West Potomac Park, Lincoln Memorial (and Vietnam Veterans Memorial), John F. Kennedy Center for the Performing Arts, the White House (south side near 15th and E streets, NW), and Arlington National Cemetery.

Old Town Trolley Tours offer an enjoyable ride around town in an old-fashioned open-sided orange-and-green trolley car. The two-hour tour makes 16 stops throughout the city, including the Pavilion at the Old Post Office Building, Washington National Cathedral, Lincoln Memorial, Hyatt Regency Hotel, Grand Hyatt, J.W. Marriott/Shops at National Place, Hotel Washington, Capitol Hilton, Holiday Inn Governor's House, Washington Hilton, Sheraton Washington, Georgetown Inn, Marbury Hotel, the Waterfront, Loews L'Enfant Plaza, and Holiday Inn Capitol Hill.

Trolleys run from 9 A.M. to 4 P.M. Labor Day to Memorial Day and 9 A.M. to 8 P.M. Memorial Day to Labor Day. The price is $11 for adults and $9 for students and senior citizens. Children under 12 ride free with an accompanying adult. Call (202) 269-3020 (recording) or (202) 269-3021.

Be sure any students in your group carry student identification cards. Although most places with admission fees have reduced prices for children, some also have lower fees for students with proper credentials.

There's no one way to organize a guidebook on different sights to be seen and enjoyed in and around Washington. I've chosen to assemble this book according to geographic areas: Capitol Hill, the Mall, the Northwest, the Southwest, the Southeast, the Northeast, Maryland, and Virginia. There are exceptions to this plan, however. I've included the Tidal Basin, Jefferson Memorial, East Potomac Park (Hains Point), the National Archives, the Bureau of Engraving and Printing, and the White House in the Mall section because the continuous green space and memorials go together.

In addition to an alphabetical index by name, there is a separate alphabetical listing grouping destinations together by category, from *A* as in airplane to *Z* as in zoo. This should be helpful if you just want to visit gardens or are looking for a public ice-skating rink.

Almost all the museums and galleries and historic tourist spots in the Washington area close by 5 or 6 P.M. However, that doesn't mean there aren't things to do in the evening. During the summer, for example, there are free public band concerts every night of the week, weather permitting. The Lincoln and Jefferson memorials are open all night, and the Washington Monument is open until midnight, so you might do the museums during the day and the memorials at night. In the evening the memorials are beautifully illuminated, the lines or crowds are smaller, and the temperature is cooler—a benefit in the summer. Grayline operates a three-hour Washington After Dark tour that departs from the terminal at 333 E Street, SW. Cost is $18 for adults and $9 for children 3 to 11. Call (301) 386-8300 for information.

Many museums, galleries, and other institutions offer memberships. These usually include a regular publication that lists upcoming events, discounts in the gift shop, discounts on admissions and programs, and other benefits. If you're visiting and you will be buying a number of items from a particular gift shop, or if you're a local resident and plan to visit one of these institutions frequently, it's probably advantageous to join. Throughout this guidebook, descriptions of institutions only will note if a membership is available. It will not detail the benefits.

Virtually all public buildings in the Washington area are wheelchair accessible. Where there is a problem, such as at the galleries around Dupont Circle, the staffs ask that you call in advance so they can assist wheelchair visitors. Other buildings that are wheelchair inaccessible are noted in the descriptive text.

Braille maps of the Capitol and the Mall can be picked up at the Sergeant-at-Arms Special Services Office in the crypt of the Capitol, at the Capitol Guide Service desk at the Rotunda, or from the Capitol Police at all public entrances to congressional office buildings. Free Metrorail maps for the visually impaired are available from the Services Office, Lighthouse for the Blind, 1421 P Street, NW, Washington, D.C. 20071; (202) 462-2900.

Washington combines the charm of a small southern town with the perils of a major metropolitan area. It is not a hellhole, but you should take normal precautions. Lock your car, secure your belongings (don't bring anything you wouldn't want to lose in the first place), and be careful about where you go, particularly at night. Be cautious about traveling alone at night or on bikepaths.

Although all of the prices given were accurate at presstime, they are, of course, subject to change. The price quoted will give you an indication that admission is in the neighborhood of $1 or $5, and any increase should still be within that range.

Similarly, tour times can change. They may vary with the season, the demand, and with the number of personnel or docents available to conduct the tours. If you are going to want a guided tour, call first to confirm the times. Even then, double check the times with the information desk when you enter a museum or gallery. I'm not paranoid; I'm just cautious and I don't like being unnecessarily disappointed.

One more word of advice. Public restrooms are scarce in Washington. In the museums they are more or less busy according to scheduled events, such as the when the crowd exits from the IMAX movie at the Air and Space Museum. There are no public toilets in the White House or in the Washington Monument. You don't want to wait in line for two hours to discover your youngster has a nature call that there's no way to answer. In other words, use the facilities whenever you can and watch the schedules so you'll know to get in line before the movie ends. When asking directions, don't always ask for the nearest restroom because it may also be the busiest. A more distant room may have no line at all and be perfectly clean and stocked.

Tourism Bureaus

The following are the addresses and phone numbers for the bureau jurisdictions around the Washington area. Some are included even though there are no specific sights mentioned from that jurisdiction. They will be helpful in assisting you locate lodgings and other attractions, such as ones you will find in the alphabetical activities list.

Washington, D.C.
Washington Convention and Visitors Association 1212 New York Avenue, NW 20005. (202) 789-7000. This is not a walk-in office. Either write or call for information before your arrival.

Washington Visitor Information Center 1455 Pennsylvania Avenue, NW 20004, in the Willard Collection of shops. The center is open 9 A.M. to 5 P.M. Monday through Saturday, and closed Sunday and federal holidays.

Maryland
Annapolis Public Information and Tourism Office City Hall, 160 Duke of Gloucester Street, Annapolis 21401. (301) 263-7940, 269-6125 (Baltimore); (301) 261-1847 (Washington, D.C.).

Anne Arundel County Tourism Council of Annapolis and Anne Arundel 6 Dock Street, Annapolis 21401. (301) 280-0445, (301) 268-TOUR.

Baltimore Area Convention and Visitors Association One East Pratt Street, Plaza level, Baltimore 21202. (301) 659-7300, (800) 343-3468.

Baltimore Area Visitors Center 300 West Pratt Street, Baltimore
21201. (301) 837-4636, (800) 282-6632.

Baltimore City Office of Promotion (for special events) 200 West
Lombard Street, Baltimore 21202. (301) 752-8632.

Baltimore County Office of Promotion and Tourism 10 Towson-
town Boulevard, East Towson 21204. (301) 887-8040.

**Calvert County Tourism Director, Department of Economic
Development** Courthouse, Prince Frederick 20678. (301) 535-4583,
(301) 855-1880.

Tourism Council of Frederick County, Inc. 19 East Church Street,
Frederick 21701. (301) 663-8687.

Howard County Tourism Council 5485 Twin Knolls Road, Columbia
21045. (301) 730-7817.

Conference and Visitors Bureau of Montgomery County, Inc. 401
Hungerford Drive, Rockville 20850. (301) 588-8687, (301) 424-1740.

Prince George's Travel Promotion Council, Inc. 8903 Presidential
Parkway, Suite 201, Upper Marlboro 20772. (301) 967-8687.

Worcester County Tourism P.O. Box 208, Snow Hill 21863. (301) 632-
3617. Or Ocean City Visitors and Convention Bureau, Inc., P.O. Box
116, Ocean City 21842. (301) 289-8181.

Virginia

**Alexandria Convention and Visitors Bureau (Ramsey House Visi-
tors Center)** 221 King Street, Alexandria 22314. (703) 838-4200.

Arlington Visitors Center 735 18th Street South, Arlington 22202.
(703) 358-5720.

Fairfax County Tourism and Convention Bureau 8300 Boone Boulevard, Suite 450 (Tysons Corner), Vienna 22182. (703) 790-3329.

Loudoun County Tourist Information Center 108D South Street, SE,
Leesburg 22075. (703) 777-9519.

Prince William County-Manassas Tourist Information Center 2231-
A Tackett's Mill Drive, Lake Ridge 22192. (703) 401-4045.

Capitol Hill

☐ United States Capitol

East end of the Mall on Capitol Hill. (202) 224-3121 (Capitol office number). Open daily 9 A.M. to 3:45 P.M. in winter, until 8 P.M. in summer. Closed Thanksgiving, Christmas, and New Year's days. Guided tours are given daily from 9 A.M. to 3:45 P.M.; call (202) 225-6827 for information. Capitol South or Union Station subway station. Tourmobile stop (First Street and Independence Avenue, SE).

Tours, lasting 45 minutes or longer during the off-season, shorter during the peak season, are given about every 15 minutes in the winter and every 5 minutes in the summer. They start in the Rotunda, beneath the white-paint-over-iron Capitol dome, and include Statuary Hall (where whispers can be heard from one side of the room to the other because of the arched ceilings), the restored old Senate and Supreme Court chambers (note that the statue of Blind Justice does not have a blindfold), the crypt area, and the Brumidi corridors in the Senate Wing (Constantino Brumidi spent 25 years creating some of the most impressive decorative art in this building).

If you neglected to write in advance to your congressional representative or senator for tickets to the chamber galleries (see Introduction), stop by his or her office to see if any are available. Foreign visitors who want tickets should apply to the office of the sergeant at arms of the Senate or the doorkeeper of the House. Committee meetings, which are listed in the daily newspaper, need no passes if they are described as open hearings.

Individual offices of representatives are on the right-hand (south) side of the Capitol, as you face it from the Mall. Senate offices are on the left (north). The Senate and House offices are connected to the Capitol by an underground subway system, which you can ride during regular tour hours.

You can tell when Congress is meeting because a flag flies over the House (when it's in session) and over the Senate (when it's in session) and a light illuminates the Goddess of Freedom statue on top of the Capitol.

From June through August, the U.S. Army, Navy, Air Force, and Marine Corps bands give free concerts on the west terrace of the

Capitol. They perform weeknights except Thursday at 8 P.M. Spectators sit on the steps.

The west lawn of the Capitol is ideal for viewing the entire Mall. Toward the left side (northwest corner) of the lawn is the sunken grotto, which is a good stop on a pleasant day. Hidden among trees and bushes, it has benches and water fountains and a mossy cave with water spraying over the rocks.

Near the statue of Ulysses S. Grant, Central Photos will take a panoramic photograph of your group, with the Capitol in the background, on a Kodak Cirkut camera that is at least 50 years old. Children particularly enjoy the fact that one person can be in the same picture twice. Because of the mechanism that operates this camera, someone can stand on the end of the group upon which the lens is first trained, and then, as the shot commences, run quickly to the other end of the group where the panoramic sweep ends. The cost is $6 for each black-and-white photo and $10 for each color photo. Usually Central Photos requires a minimum of 15 people, but they will take your picture if your group is smaller. You must, however, buy a minimum of ten pictures. The photographer is at the statue from 9 A.M. to 3 P.M. Monday through Saturday, from mid-March to mid- or late-June (the busy group season in Washington). It's best to call (202) 544-6065 for an appointment; photos can be taken any time of the year.

The Ulysses S. Grant Memorial, dedicated to the soldiers who fought in the Civil War, is great for climbing on.

On the east side of the Capitol you can usually catch a television camera crew doing a "stand-up" report for the evening news.

There is a public restaurant on the Senate side where you can try the famous bean soup ($1.10). It's open from 11:30 A.M. to 3:30 P.M.

☐ **Library of Congress**

10 First Street, SE (First and East Capitol streets). (202) 707-5000. Open Monday through Friday 8:30 A.M. to 9:30 P.M., Saturday 8:30 A.M. to 5 P.M., and Sunday 1 to 5 P.M. Closed Christmas and New Year's days. Thirty-minute tours are given daily in the James Madison Building (101 Independence Avenue, SE) at 10 A.M., 10:30 A.M., 1 P.M., and 1:30 P.M.; call (202) 707-5458 for tour information. Capitol South subway station.

The three buildings in this complex—the James Madison, the Thomas Jefferson, and the John Adams—hold the largest library collection in the world. Contrary to popular belief, however, the library does not house a copy of every book that's ever been printed, not even every book that's been printed in English or in the United States. It does contain one of the three remaining copies of the Gutenberg vellum

Bibles (1455), 575 miles of bookshelves, and 90,500,000 items in a collection that grows daily. According to library estimates, 26 million books, 10 million prints and photos, and 80,000 films are stored here.

The Jefferson Building is under restoration and will not be completely reopened until 1992. In the meantime, tours are given of the Madison Building and can be tailored to children if you let them know you're coming. Children like the atrium with its trees, the Maps Division, and a small fourth-floor exhibit about copyrights that includes some Disney characters and the first Barbie and Ken dolls. The exhibit is open 8:30 A.M. to 5 P.M. weekdays. A 20-minute film on the scope and size of the collection is shown every half hour in Room 139 of the Madison Building.

There are some extraordinary collections, such as the Music Division with its 1,500 hundred flutes and five Stradivarius violins, the Houdini papers, the Asian Division, and the European Room, which claims the largest library of Russian books in the West. But these are open only to scholars; your older children may qualify if they are doing a research project on one of these subjects.

Changing exhibits can be found in the Madison Building, and in the Jefferson when it reopens.

Free concerts are presented about twice a month, usually on Thursday and Friday nights from October through December and from February through April. Until the renovations are complete at the Jefferson Building, the concerts are presented at the National Academy of Sciences Auditorium (said to be one of the most acoustically perfect spaces in the city), 21st and C streets, NW. These 90-minute chamber music concerts are first-come, first-served and start at 8 P.M. They are performed by the Juilliard String Quartet and the Beaux Arts Trio, who are the artists in residence. Call (202) 707-5502 (recording) for information.

☐ **Supreme Court of the United States**

1 First Street, NE. (202) 479-3000. Open Monday through Friday 9 A.M. to 4:30 P.M. Closed weekends and federal holidays. When the Court is not in session, courtroom lectures, covering the history and functions of the Court and defining an oral argument are presented every hour on the half hour from 9:30 A.M. to 3:30 P.M. Cafeteria hours are 7:15 to 10:30 A.M., 11:30 A.M. to 2 P.M. Snack Bar hours are 10:30 A.M. to 3:30 P.M. Capitol South or Union Station subway station.

The highest court in the land is open to the public on a limited basis. Because most people only see the Court as nine robed justices who hand down decisions on the Constitution during television coverage, a personal visit is impressive. The Court hears oral arguments at

10 A.M., 11 A.M., 1 P.M., and 2 P.M. on Monday, Tuesday, and Wednesday for approximately two weeks of each month starting the first Monday in October and continuing through April. During May and June, the Court convenes at 10 A.M. to deliver opinions.

There are no regular guided tours, but you may tour the building on your own. When the Court is in session, there are two lines to enter the courtroom. One line is for people who want to sit through all or part of the entire session. The sessions are open to the public on a first-come, first-served basis. The other queue is a three-minute line for visitors who just want to see the chambers. You can also write to your congressional representative for a special 2 P.M. weekday tour that includes the East and West Conference rooms (if they're not in use for a meeting or reception), plus a glimpse into the capacious and solemn oak-paneled law library.

A 20-minute film that details the activities of the Court is shown continuously. Rotating exhibits downstairs tell a coherent tale of the historical significance of what goes on upstairs. A Supreme Court Historical Society kiosk is on the ground floor. Take a look at the cantilevered marble spiral staircase directly across from the women's room, at the Maryland Avenue basement level. You can't walk on the steps, but you can see them.

☐ Folger Shakespeare Library and Theatre

201 East Capitol Street, SE. (202) 546-4000 (theater), (202) 544-4600 (library), (202) 544-7077 (concerts). The library is open daily 10 A.M. to 4 P.M. Closed federal holidays and on Sunday from Labor Day to April 15. Guided tours of the Great Hall are given from 11 A.M. to 1 P.M. Union Station or Capitol South subway station.

This multifaceted operation contains a theater, a library, the Great Hall, and the Consort. Henry Clay Folger, a late-19th-century student at Amherst College in Massachusetts and one-time chairman of the board of Standard Oil Company, was the stimulus for this library and the indoor version of an outdoor playhouse. The theater is more properly called the Elizabethan Theatre, in honor of Queen Elizabeth, the Virgin Queen, but almost everyone refers to it as the Folger Theatre. The resident company specializes in presenting the works of Shakespeare and his contemporaries.

Free docent-led guided tours of the Great Hall (with the names of all of Shakespeare's plays around the room) can last 15 or 30 minutes, depending on your interests. Changing exhibits are explained, and there is always a 1632 First Folio of all of Shakespeare's works on display. If the theater is not in use for rehearsal, it can be included in the tour.

The Folger Shakespeare Library itself is for scholarly research only, and then only by those with previously approved credentials.

The Folger's Education Department programs festivals for high-school students in the spring, with sword-fighting demonstrations, slides shows, and other activities. Call to see if you can join them.

From October through May, a musical series that features medieval, renaissance, and baroque compositions is scheduled on Saturday, Sunday, and Monday evenings and Sunday afternoon. Many different types of early instruments are played, and there's always at least one singer. On occasion, the musicians are even dressed in period costumes. The Saturday and Sunday concerts are given in the Great Hall, the Monday night concert in the theater, and the December concerts are given in the Washington National Cathedral. The Sunday night concerts are preceded by a one-hour conversation led by local radio personality Robert Aubry Davis. He talks with the musicians and the audience about the evening's music selections. The experience is accessible to almost every age. Tickets are $16 for the evening concerts and $13.50 for the Sunday matinee concert, with a 10 percent discount for children and seniors.

The gift shop is strong on renaissance souvenirs, including coloring books, children's books, games, note cards, puzzles, unicorns, and T-shirts.

The Mall

This section takes the visitor from the east end of the Mall, by the Capitol, about 1 1/4 miles westward to the Lincoln Memorial.

The Mall is the stretch of green parkland that runs between Constitution and Independence avenues. At one end is the Capitol. It perches on a rise about 90 feet above sea level (thus the name Capitol Hill). At the other end is the Lincoln Memorial. On either side are galleries and museums and other interesting government buildings. There is no general admission charge to these institutions, and only occasionally is there a small fee for a specific exhibit. Periodically, a traveling exhibit will be so popular that timed-entry tickets will be distributed. These arrangements are listed in the local papers.

With one exception, we'll travel first along Independence Avenue, and then along Constitution.

Enjoy the Mall. It is an accessible, "please touch" park. You may walk on it, play frisbee, take a sunbath, or people-watch. National Park Police patrol the area on horseback and take time to talk with the children. The Mall fills to near-capacity during the all-day festivities on the Fourth of July. In the same month, the Smithsonian holds the annual Folk Life Festival celebrating the culture, crafts, and traditions of various communities. The festival usually features one state and one country. It fills up several blocks of the Mall, so you can experience cooking demonstrations, dancing, native crafts, storytelling, and whatever may be indigenous to the areas represented.

The Mall is home to a 1940 Allan Herschell-model carousel with 58 horses and boats. It spins its merry way and its merry tunes from May to September, 10:30 A.M. to 5 P.M. weekends, 10:30 A.M. to 4:30 P.M. weekdays. A three-minute ride costs only 75 cents.

For a long time, Uncle Beasley, a fiber-glass triceratops sitting in front of the Museum of Natural History, was a favorite for child climbing. But some children fell off and were injured, so museum personnel started looking for a softer ground surface. Then they realized Uncle Beasley has been sinking. For the meantime, Uncle Beasley is off-limits, but should be relocated sometime in the near future.

There are five subway stations very convenient to the Mall, plus a couple that are less convenient, depending upon which building you'll be visiting. Do not automatically go to the Smithsonian subway station, particularly if you're visiting the Botanic Gardens (Federal Center SW station is closer) or the Air and Space Museum (L'Enfant Plaza station is closer). The station nearest to each sight is included in the description.

We will begin with our exception, a visit to "The Castle."

☐ Smithsonian Institution Building

Tenth Street and Jefferson Drive. (202) 357-2700 for all questions about various Smithsonian operations. Open daily 9 A.M. to 5:30 P.M. Closed Christmas Day. Membership available. Smithsonian subway station.

For your initial or refresher course on what is in which museum or what you want to see, stop by The Castle, the original Smithsonian Building and now the visitor center for the institution. It opens at 9 A.M., an hour before the museums and galleries, so you have plenty of time to watch a 20-minute film (with captioning and audio loop), explore the touch-screen interactive video monitors, and talk with the information guides. Here's the place to ask what the Hope Diamond is worth, how to get to the National Zoo, or where to find a tobacco hornworm. Information is available in English, Arabic, Chinese, French, German, Spanish, and Japanese. Not all the buildings along the Mall are part of the Smithsonian (such as the National Gallery of Art), but the experts here will provide information on those buildings as well as their own.

The mausoleum for James Smithson, who left the funding for the Smithsonian, is in the front left lobby. Smithson was an English chemist and mineralogist who died in 1829 and bequeathed money to the United States "to found at Washington, D.C., under the name of Smithsonian Institution, an establishment for the increase and diffusion of knowledge among men." The mineral smithsonite is named after him. His body was brought over following his death, for he never visited this country while he was alive.

Now, to start our Mall tour.

☐ United States Botanic Garden

Maryland Avenue, near First Street. (202) 225-8333. Open daily 9 A.M. to 5 P.M., until 9 P.M. in summer. Closed Christmas and New Year's days. Guided tours with advance notice. Free horticulture classes and lectures September through June. Federal Center SW subway station.

Children who've never left their own climate before will be fascinated by the different biomes represented here. There are subtropical plants (orchids and ficus trees), bromeliads (Spanish moss and pineapple plant), ferns (the vessel fern, thought to be the oldest plant in the garden), cacti (agave and barrel), more than 300 palms, and even an economics section (citrus and chocolate trees are examples of plants with an economic value) to illustrate that trees are for more than shade and a great place to put a secret clubhouse.

More than 10,000 species and varieties of plants tempt your eyes and your nose, including the bunyabunya tree from Australia, the lychee tree from China, the tapioca plant from Brazil, and the Arabian coffee tree.

Each season has its own show, which might include 90 varieties of azaleas or an extensive orchid collection. The annual Easter exhibit has thousands of spring blooms. The Christmas greenery display features 3,000 poinsettia plants.

☐ National Air and Space Museum

Independence Avenue between Fourth and Seventh streets. (202) 357-2700, (202) 357-1686 (recording about Langley Theater presentations). Open daily 10 A.M. to 5:30 P.M. Closed Christmas Day. Free hour-long highlights tours are given at 10:15 A.M. and 1 P.M. Membership available. Tourmobile stop. L'Enfant Plaza subway station.

The museum's two theaters must be mentioned first, because if you plan to visit them you should buy your time-specific tickets as you enter the museum, then tour until your theater time. Tickets are $2.25 for adults and $1.25 for children, students, and senior citizens for each show at both the Samuel P. Langley IMAX Theater and the Albert Einstein Planetarium.

At the IMAX theater, several large-format aviation films are shown daily. They give viewers the feeling that they are as close to flying or being out in space as they'll ever get without setting a foot off the earth. The screen is five stories high and seven stories wide, or 50 by 75 feet. *To Fly!* takes viewers from one coast of America to the other, swooping down through the Grand Canyon, along cliffs, and over cities and farms. *The Dream is Alive* is about the astronauts of four space-shuttle missions. Both now have audio descriptions via special headsets to help partially sighted and blind theater patrons comprehend the action of the film. During pauses in the film's regular narration and dialogue, a second narrator describes exactly what is being shown on the screen. This audio description is the work of Metropolitan Washington Ear, Inc., where Cody and Margaret Pfanstiehl are the inspirations behind this worthwhile project.

The Albert Einstein Planetarium show is screened every 40 minutes, except on Tuesday and Thursday when the three midday shows are replaced by free Noontime with the Stars lectures. The show is recommended for ages ten and up; the lectures are suitable for older children.

Air and Space is the most visited museum in the world, with as many as 10 million people walking through its doors each year. Although much of the aviation history took place before today's children were born, almost all of it took place during the lifetime of today's grandparents, so this "ancient history" actually is quite current. What are your first memories of flight? How do they compare with today's supersonic and intergalactic ships? What are your children's first memories of flight? When it comes to basics, though, the children don't seem nearly as interested in that miraculous concept of gravity defying action as they do in how astronauts eat, sleep, and go to the bathroom.

The museum has published a guide for younger visitors, available at the information desk, which lists 11 stops, all suitable for pre- schoolers.

Among the museum's highlights are the Voyager (the flying fuel tank that made the first nonstop, unrefueled flight around the world in 1986, piloted by Dick Rutan and Jena Yeager—talk about tight quarters), the Wright Brothers' original Kitty Hawk Flyer (which didn't fly any higher than it's hanging in the museum now), the X-1 (first aircraft to break the sound barrier flown by Chuck Yeager), and a Skylab orbital workshop that children (even grown-up children) can walk through to examine the astronauts' living and lab quarters (the line tends to be very long during peak season).

A must-see for any age is the S.S. *Pussiewillow II*, in Gallery 211 on the second floor, one of several fantastic creations of artist Rowland Emmett. This flying machine is made of badminton birdies, bicycle wheels, chandeliers, clothesline pulleys, floral carpets, and other ordinary household objects. It tilts, spins, flaps, and captivates. You can't actually enjoy the chocolate-chip cookies being offered by the "wiry" pilot, Dr. Leo Capricorn, because the whole scene is behind plastic. You can, however, enjoy this flight of imagination in this flight museum. Most people are familiar with Emmett's enterprising genius because of the numerous strange vehicles he designed for the movie *Chitty Chitty Bang Bang*.

Future women aviators and astronauts may be interested in several displays, including the bright red Lockheed Vega that Amelia Earhart flew across the Atlantic in 1932 (the first woman to fly solo across the Atlantic) and wonder at its innocence. Also on the second floor is a plane flown by Charles and Anne Morrow Lindbergh when she was serving as her husband's navigator and radio operator on preliminary flights to survey possible overseas routes. Astronaut Sally Ride's flight suit is here. Children's books about Earhart and other women aviators are on sale in the museum shop.

The 800-seat Flight Line cafeteria and the 180-seat Wright Place full-service restaurant (with sandwiches called The Titan I and the Apollo 8) are located at the east end of the museum, providing a great view of the Capitol.

Free special-interest lectures, demonstrations, films, and displays on aviation, the skies, and space exploration are scheduled regularly. For a free events calendar write Calendar, Room 3363, NASM, Washington, D.C. 20560. Many of these events are in the evening, after the museum has closed.

☐ Hirschhorn Museum and Sculpture Garden

Eighth Street and Independence Avenue. (202) 357-2700. Open daily 10 A.M. to 5:30 P.M. Closed Christmas Day. Guided walk-in tours of about 45 to 60 minutes are given Monday through Saturday at 10:30 A.M., 12 noon, and 1:30 P.M., (except on the third Tuesday of the month when there is no 10:30 A.M. tour); and on Sunday at 12:30 P.M., 1:30 P.M., 2:30 P.M., and 3:30 P.M. A 12-minute slide show that introduces the collection is screened continuously in the orientation room on the lower level from 10 A.M. to 5 P.M. daily. Special tours for children and groups, sculpture tours for the visually impaired, and sign-language tours for the hearing impaired should be arranged a month in advance by calling (202) 357-3235. L'Enfant Plaza subway station.

This doughnut-shaped building is designed to show huge works on the outer, windowless walls, and smaller pieces along the inner circle. The Hirschhorn, the modern gallery in the Smithsonian group, displays paintings and sculptures by Rodin, Calder, Eakins, Matisse, Davis, Stella, and Estes.

Children's films, from cartoon and mainstream, such as a Babar tale and *The Little Mermaid,* to the avant-garde, are screened on Saturdays at 11 A.M. throughout the school year. Program subjects vary and are not necessarily related to the museum exhibits. The films generally are of most interest to 6 to 12 year olds.

The outdoor sculpture garden is a great place for a relaxing break, but remind the children that these sculptures are not for climbing.

☐ Arts and Industries Building

900 Jefferson Drive. (202) 357-2700, (202) 357-1500 (Discovery Theater reservations, voice or TDD). Open daily 10 A.M. to 5:30 P.M. Closed Christmas Day. Walk-in tours given as staff or docents are available, usually only on Saturday. Tourmobile stop. Smithsonian subway station.

Arts and Industries is to the United States of a century ago what Epcot and World's Fairs are to our future. In fact, most of the exhibits here came from the 1876 Philadelphia Centennial Exposition, which showed items from the 37 states that were then in the Union, plus goods from several countries. There are wings dedicated to machinery, military equipment, furniture, and technology. Displays show-case U.S. Patent Office models, manufactured goods, and machinery of the Victorian age. The objects range from silver services to a beauti-fully restored locomotive engine and Liberty Bell replicas made from tobacco, sugar, and stone. A central rotunda has a fountain and changing floral displays.

Discovery Theater presents live theatrical performances for young people and their families. The 45- to 60-minute presentations, which may be about Sojourner Truth (a 19th-century abolitionist, reformer, and freed slave who traveled widely preaching emancipation and women's rights), West African folktales, Beatrix Potter stories, or dance, are addressed to children groups from prekindergarten to ninth grade. Promotional literature about the programs includes the appropriate age group with the description of each production. Show times are 10 A.M. and 11:30 A.M. Tuesday through Friday and 11:30 A.M. and 1 P.M. on Saturday. Admission is $3.50 for adults and $3 for children 12 and under. The theater is closed on Thanksgiving and around Christmas and New Year's days.

☐ Enid A. Haupt Garden

Tenth Street and Independence Avenue. (202) 357-1926. Open daily 7 A.M. to 8 P.M. in summer, 7 A.M. to 5:45 P.M. in winter. Smithsonian subway station.

Part of the Quadrangle, immediately south of The Castle, this terrific spot for a respite includes a formal Victorian parterre, the Moongate Garden with two nine-foot-tall moongates and pools shaded by weeping cherry trees, and the Fountain Garden with a waterfall and thornless hawthorns.

The Arthur M. Sackler Gallery and the National Museum of African Art of the Smithsonian Institution are unique for a couple of reasons, but perhaps their most unusual aspect is that they both are three stories underground, beneath the Enid A. Haupt Garden. They are entered from two pavilions in the garden: The Sackler access adjoins the Moongate Garden; the African art museum is entered from the Fountain Garden. Each entrance is topped by large skylights that allow daylight to flood down the wide staircases to the bottom floors some 57 feet below. (Elevators are also available, and are interesting because the floors are labeled G, 1, 2, and 3, as you descend. The idea of floor numbers increasing as an elevator goes down is an odd concept.) The two museums are connected again on the lower level, so you don't have to return to the surface to go from one to another, although you may want to for a relaxing break between the two distinctly different exhibitions. Consider combining a visit to the

Sackler with one to the nearby Freer Gallery for a comprehensive visit to the world of Asian art.

☐ Arthur M. Sackler Gallery

1050 Independence Avenue. (202) 357-2700, (202) 357-2041, (202) 357-4886 (Education Department). Open daily 10 A.M. to 5:30 P.M. Closed Christmas Day. Hour-long guided walk-in tours are given Monday through Friday at 10:30 A.M., 11:30 A.M., 12 noon, and 1:30 P.M.; weekends 11:30 A.M. and 1:30 P.M. Guided group tours must be arranged in advance. Smithsonian subway station.

The Sackler contains a permanent collection of art from China, the ancient Near East, and South Asia and Southeast Asia. Included are objects in bronze, jade, silver, gold, lacquer, and ceramic, as well as paintings and sculpture that span the period between 4000 B.C. and the 20th century. The museum also houses a major collection of Persian and Indian manuscripts and paintings, and a selection of Japanese works, along with changing exhibits. Look for the pamphlets that provide brief, illustrated texts for each exhibit.

Regularly scheduled workshops, storytelling events, and other activities, some of which may be appropriate for children, are listed in the monthly calendar. Group tours (classes from kindergarten on up, scout troops) are scheduled a month ahead of time and are tailored to specific interests and fields of study. They may include a hands-on tour and activity sheets. Call the Education Department to see if one is scheduled and if you may join it.

☐ National Museum of African Art

950 Independence Avenue. (202) 357-2700, (202) 357-4860 (Education Department). Open daily 10 A.M. to 5:30 P.M. Closed Christmas Day. Introductory tours (about 45 minutes) are given Monday, Thursday, and Friday at 10:30 A.M.; Tuesday and Wednesday at 10:30 A.M. and 1:30 P.M.; and weekends at 10:30 A.M., 1:30 P.M., and 3:30 P.M. Group tour requests should be made by mail three months in advance. African folktale storytelling for children takes place on Saturday at 1 P.M.; no reservations needed. Smithsonian subway station.

The museum, which focuses on the collection, study, and exhibition of the traditional arts of sub-Saharan Africa, is the only institution of its kind in the country. Its permanent collection of bronze, wood, ivory, cast metal, and ceramic objects is an important resource for the study of African art and culture. These works share gallery space with changing exhibitions. Nice to note is the use of large color photographs to illuminate what purpose masks, statues, and divination boards serve in African culture.

☐ Freer Gallery of Art

12th Street and Jefferson Drive. (202) 357-2700. Closed for renovation and restoration until at least the fall of 1992. The gallery, when reopened, should resume its schedule of walk-in tours Monday through Saturday at 10:30 A.M., Sunday at 1:30 P.M. Smithsonian subway station.

Charles Lang Freer donated the collection of oriental and American art that fills this gallery. Freer's friend, James McNeill Whistler, created the Peacock Room, the highlight here for many children because of its striking visual impact. Other treasures include Buddhist sculpture, early Biblical manuscripts, Chinese jades and bronzes, paintings, Japanese screens, and Indian miniatures. The vast collection has regularly changing displays, but Freer's will stipulated that items in the collection may not leave the gallery, nor may other objects be displayed.

☐ Bureau of Engraving and Printing

14th and C streets, SW. (202) 447-1391, (202) 447-9709 (recording). Open Monday through Friday 9 A.M. to 2 P.M. Closed weekends, federal holidays, and December 24 through January 2. Twenty-minute self-guided tours begin at the 14th Street entrance. Guided tours are offered from early June through late August. Tourmobile stop. Smithsonian subway station.

This is one of the most popular sights in the area, so arrive early (particularly March through September) to avoid long lines and major disappointment. Bureau personnel will close the line early to assure all in line can enter by 2 P.M.

All of the nation's paper money (the paper is produced by the Crane Paper Company) is designed, engraved, and printed here, along with bonds, 30 billion postage stamps a year, White House invitations, and several hundred other items you'll learn about in the introductory film. About 22 million bills are printed daily and about $60 trillion are printed every year in $1, $5, and $10 denominations. Larger bills—$20, $50, $100—are printed less frequently. The largest bills—$500, $1,000, $5,000, $10,000—have not been printed for many years. This is the only bureau that prints paper money; coins are minted in Denver and Philadelphia.

You'll walk past exhibits about counterfeit money, printing methods, outdated currency, and you'll see presses working, machines cutting and stacking the bills, and money being checked. You are separated from the actual printing process by thick glass windows. The beginning of this tour can be a little dull, but there's no denying that seeing all that money being printed, examined, cut, and packaged is fascinating. After the tour, enter the visitor center and a gift shop where you can purchase shredded currency and uncut blocks of currency. Several signs and recorded announcements respond to the inevitable statement about free samples.

Now, on the other side of the Mall, along Constitution Avenue, again starting from the Capitol end, you'll find the following buildings.

☐ National Gallery of Art

Sixth Street at Constitution Avenue. (202) 842-6358, (202) 737-4215 (recording). Open Monday through Saturday 10 A.M. to 5 P.M., Sunday 11 A.M. to 6 P.M. Closed Christmas and New Year's days. West Building walk-in tours (about one hour) are given Monday through Saturday at 3 P.M. and Sunday at 1 P.M. East Building walk-in tours are given Monday through Friday at 11:30 A.M., Saturday at 11 A.M., and Sunday at 12 noon. Terrific gift shops. Tourmobile stop. Archives subway station.

The gallery, which is not part of the Smithsonian, is comprised of two buildings, the West (or Main) Building and the East Building. The West Building houses pre-20th century art. Across the National Gallery Plaza in the East Building are 20th-century artworks.

When your children start talking about those Teenage Mutant Ninja Turtles, you can show them two of the artists, Raphael and Leonardo. The gallery has a Donatello drawing in its print collection and you can set up an appointment to see it. There's no help for your Michelangelo though.

Major European and American artists are represented in the West Building, including Raphael (Gallery 8) and Leonardo da Vinci (Gallery 6; the only da Vinci in the western hemisphere).

There are a number of special programs for children and families. You can take the free self-guided tour; a book is available in the gift shop that helps explain the paintings, or you can pick up a free brochure. Special exhibitions usually are accompanied by special tours and activities for children six to ten years old. Call the Education Department for the schedule (202) 842-6249, or ask to be put on the mailing list by writing to the National Gallery of Art, Washington, D.C. 20565.

Tours also are available for children from three or four years old all the way through high-school age. Many of these organized tours are scout or classroom groups, but you "qualify" as a group even if it's a birthday party. In fact, the staff will happily organize a special tour for those with specific interests. As an example, if your group wants to study the depiction of a certain subject, such as weather, in the artworks, then the staff will create that tour for you. These are all conversational tours and can include items from the permanent or touring exhibits, from either the West Building or the East Building.

Many children seem to have fun just walking by the cascade in the passageway connecting the two buildings.

☐ National Archives

Constitution Avenue between Seventh and Ninth streets. (202) 501-5000 (recorded information about special programs). Open daily 10 A.M. to 9 P.M. April 1 through Labor Day, 10 A.M. to 5:30 P.M. the rest of the year. Closed Christmas Day. Guided tours are given Monday through Friday by appointment only; call (202) 501-5205 for reservations. The Pennsylvania Avenue entrance provides access to the Central Research and Microfilm Research rooms, open Monday through Friday 8:45 A.M. to 10 P.M. and Saturday 9 A.M. to 5 P.M. Closed federal holidays. Call (202) 501-5400 for research information. Archives subway station.

America's most revered documents are stored here, including all four pages of the Declaration of Independence, the Constitution, and the Bill of Rights. They are kept in sealed glass-and-bronze cases filled with protective helium. During the day two of the pages of the Declaration of Independence, the Constitution, and the Bill of Rights are on display. At night the cases are lowered into a bomb- and fireproof vault 20 feet below floor level. On September 17, Constitution Day (the anniversary of the presentation of the Constitution), all four pages of the Declaration of Independence are available for viewing. There's also a 1297 copy of the Magna Carta.

Among the many other documents in the collection are 3.2 billion textual documents, 1.6 million cartographic items, 5.2 million still photographs, 9.7 million aerial photographs, 110,000 reels of motion picture film, and 173,000 video and sound recordings.

Summertime children's programs include a film series, lectures, special activities, and exhibits. Call (202) 523-3347 for information.

Serious genealogy research is done here, plus students also may research term papers on such diverse subjects as the Civil War photographs of Mathew Brady, Tokyo Rose's World War II radio propaganda tapes, land claims by Indian tribes, passenger ship manifests, the 1963 Civil Rights March on Washington, or the Watergate tapes.

Next to the National Archives, on the Pennsylvania Avenue side, is a small white marble block dedicated to President Franklin D. Roosevelt, who supposedly said he did not want a monument built to him that was larger than his desk.

☐ Museum of Natural History

Tenth Street between Constitution Avenue and Madison Drive. (202) 357-2700. Open daily 10 A.M. to 5:30 P.M. Closed Christmas Day. Guided tours (about 45 minutes) are offered Monday, Tuesday, Thursday, Friday, and

Sunday at 10:30 A.M.; daily at 1:30 P.M. Scorpion and hairy tarantula feedings are weekends at 11:30 A.M., 12:30 P.M., and 1:30 P.M. (reconfirm times at the information desk). During peak season and on many weekends, free timed tickets are sometimes issued for the Discovery Room and the Insect Zoo; check at the information desk. Tourmobile stop. Federal Triangle or Archives subway station.

Greeting you, as you enter from the Madison Drive entrance, is the largest African bush elephant ever shot. He stands three stories high, is 13 feet tall, weighed 12 tons, and had 24-inch foot tracks. Two huge (30 feet and 40 feet) totem poles carved by the Haida Indians, and one pole carved by the Tsimshian Indians, tribes native to the Pacific Northwest, guard the east stairwell of the building. From there you can venture into any corner and find everything in the natural sciences, all the way down to the tiniest little insects.

And it's the Insect Zoo that particularly excites children. Want to watch tarantulas being fed? How about petting a live Madagascar hissing cockroach or stroking a fat, green tobacco hornworm? Would you find a one-foot-long centipede slightly intimidating? Well, this is the place to become friendly with the little critters. Children love it. Fortunately, for adults, if the children are under 12, they must be accompanied by an adult. Fortunately, because adults love it too.

Other exhibits include animals from all parts of the world, in realistic settings. Among the skillfully executed displays is one of birds in flight and one of special-interest birds, such as the Antarctic penguin, the pheasant with its enormous colored plumes, and the ostrich, complete with just-hatched babies.

Dinosaurs used to roam this land, and you can see reconstructed dinosaur skeletons here. Dioramas show these animals in their natural habitats and flying reptile reconstructions hang on the nearby walls.

In the Naturalist Center, it's time for hands-on learning, with its drawers full of minerals and arrowheads, and its ready-to-use microscopes.

About halfway through the Hall of Mineral Sciences, you'll see the Hope Diamond, the largest blue diamond in the world. Then there's the 330-carat sapphire known as the Star of India. And besides them, there are hundreds, if not thousands of other mineral examples in virtually every hue and every size.

In addition to the big gift shop, which offers such wonders as gems, fossils, and arrowheads (at reasonable prices), there's a Dinostore that only carries dinosaur-related items, including cookie cutters, decorated wearing apparel, models, and puzzles.

☐ National Museum of American History

14th Street between Constitution Avenue and Madison Drive. (202) 357-2700. Open daily 10 A.M. to 5:30 P.M. Closed Christmas Day. Hour-long walk-in highlights tours are scheduled Monday through Friday at 10 A.M., 11 A.M., 1 P.M., and 1:30 P.M.; Saturday at 10 A.M., 11 A.M., and 1 P.M.; check at the information desk about Sunday tours. Ceremonial Court tours are given weekdays at 10:30 A.M., 12:30 P.M., and 1:30 P.M. Times and topics of regular tours, concerts, lectures, films, and other activities are posted at the information desks, which are staffed daily 10 A.M. to 4 P.M. Tourmobile stop. Smithsonian subway station.

This ten-acre compilation devoted to the exhibition, care, and study of artifacts that reflect the experience of the American people can be daunting and easily take a day or more, so here are some of the highlights. The first thing you see when you come in from the Mall entrance is the crowd of people hanging over a circular railing. This overlook affords a view of the large Foucault pendulum, which demonstrates the rotation of the earth.

Among the national treasures on view is the original Star-Spangled Banner, the flag that Francis Scott Key saw the night he wrote our national anthem. It is displayed every hour on the half hour during a short sound-and-light show. The inaugural gowns of the seven living first ladies are on exhibit in the Ceremonial Court; the rest of the dresses are being restored and should return to the exhibition in late 1991. Some presidential memorabilia, White House china, and decorative art objects also are on display in the court. Other treasures, which may not be national in scope but are of historic interest, are a 19th-century post office, Archie Bunker's chair, Judy Garland's ruby slippers from the *Wizard of Oz,* and Howdy Doody.

The Ceremonial Court also is where children can view a collection of toys from the 1830s forward. They belonged to White House children and grandchildren, and include a wooden chest of travel games from Thomas "Tad" Lincoln, and a gathering of ragtag well-loved Teddy bears named after Theodore Roosevelt who once shied at shooting a bear cub.

Other interesting exhibits are display cases filled with hidden and trick cameras concealed in lighters, opera glasses, shoe heels, and even a lacy black garter. You can "write with light": Place your hand, face, or a favorite toy dinosaur on a counter, push a button, and a shadow impression of the image appears.

Photography equipment, from the earliest still cameras and a primitive darkroom setup to today's motorized equipment, captures the attention and interest of many children.

The five-storied Doll House, which reflects life at the turn of the century, is always a favorite with children. Its 22 rooms, including parlors, bedrooms, and guest rooms, are outfitted with all sorts of grown-up furnishings in miniature, such as a fish tank in the living room and a typewriter in the study.

One hands-on exhibit that lives up to its name is Hands-on History. It gives young carpenters the opportunity to assemble a Chippendale chair or a wooden barrel. This room is so popular that free timed passes are sometimes issued to control the crowds.

Transformers are not a phenomenon of the 1980s; we've been "transforming" things throughout our history, although not in quite the same manner. A Material World shows how we have transformed such everyday natural resources as wood into various functional tools or clay into earthenware coffee cups. One of the stars for children in this exhibit is the low-slung Swamp Rat 30A. It was the first dragster to exceed 270 miles per hour in the quarter mile (1986) and has perhaps 60 different and distinct materials in its construction. Another interesting stop is a hands-on display of a ten-foot, 17-ton section of a main cable from the George Washington Bridge that has 26,474 individual steel strands.

If you haven't visited the Bureau of Engraving and Printing, you can see all kinds of money here. The exhibit tells the whole story, from primitive bartering with beads and shells to our present complex monetary system. There is a lumpy-looking Lydian coin from 65 B.C. and a $100,000 bill bearing the likeness of President Wilson.

Transportation takes up space, too, and features enormous train engines (take note of the photographs by Jack Bittner that show how the engine was moved into the building). Other rail-related objects are Southern Railway's Pacific-type passenger engine; the Seattle cable car of 1888; the 1836 eight-wheel passenger car, the oldest in existence; a diorama of New York's Third Avenue el as it looked in 1880; and a collection of scale models showing the development of rail transportation.

Automobile enthusiasts will want to pause to look at the first Duryea (1893), a 1894 Haynes, a 1903 Oldsmobile, and a 1913 Ford Model T. Computer buffs will like the adding and calculating machines and the various data-processing devices in the Physical Sciences and Mathematics Section.

Demonstrations of how laser and maser beams work are among the displays illustrating the development and application of electricity theories. Scientists of tomorrow can observe and study the contributions to science made by Benjamin Franklin, Michael Faraday, and others.

The importance of petroleum and the role of the petrochemical industry in modern society are presented through a description of the methods and equipment used to discover, drill, recover, refine, and transport petroleum.

The list of exhibits continues, with navigational equipment, musical instruments from the 18th and 19th centuries, and the combination country store and post office that operated in Headsville, West Virginia, from 1861 to 1914. It still serves as a post office and your mail deposited here will have a cancellation stamp that reads "Smithsonian Station."

☐ **Washington Monument**

The Mall between 15th and 17th streets. (202) 426-6839. Open daily 8 A.M. to 12 midnight April through Labor Day, 9 A.M. to 5 P.M. the first Tuesday in September through March. Expect to wait 45 minutes for every circle of tourists in line around the monument. Tourmobile stop. Smithsonian subway station.

Take the elevator up to the observation deck at the 500-foot level for the four-way view of the city. From the two north windows you can see the Ellipse and the White House, from the east the Mall Area and the Capitol, from the south the Tidal Basin and Jefferson Memorial, and from the west the Reflecting Pool and Lincoln Memorial. For nighttime viewing, the lights at the White House go out at 11 P.M. and Jefferson and Lincoln are illuminated until midnight.

The elevator takes 70 seconds to ascend, 60 seconds to descend, and the last elevator departure is ten minutes before closing (11:50 P.M. in the summer and 4:50 P.M. in the winter).

If a staff member is available to lead, you can walk down the 897 steps with a guided tour. During the 45-minute descent, you will hear tales about the wonderful walls, which include 193 ornately inscribed blocks of marble dedicated to President Washington. They came from various cities, states, fire companies (showing firefighters in action), train companies (an entire train), and countries, such as Japan, Turkey, Siam (now Thailand), Greece, and Switzerland. There are 50 landings, no windows, and the upper portion of the monument is a little narrow. If you can't take the tour, you can see some of the stones through the elevator window (next to the elevator operator) as the ride goes up and down the monument. You are not allowed to walk up the steps.

Many activities are scheduled at the Sylvan Theater (southeast corner at Independence Avenue and 15th Street) on the monument grounds. As with any outdoor venue, performance schedules are subject to the weather. Listen to the radio stations for notice of cancellation.

Prime summertime activities at the theater are concerts performed by military bands, big bands, and other music groups usually on

Tuesday, Wednesday, Friday, and Sunday at 7:30 P.M. The evening may feature such local singing stars Karen Henderson with the Trux Baldwin Orchestra. Bring a picnic and a blanket or lawn chairs and celebrate a summer evening with music and dance.

You'll probably spend some time in line waiting to go up the monument. If you're queuing during the early evening hours, however, you will be entertained by the music groups playing at the Sylvan Theater.

A boomerang competition is held on the monument grounds every spring, preceded by instructions in making and throwing the boomerang. There is a moderate charge for instructions, but no entry fee for the competition.

The Fourth of July concert that used to feature the Beach Boys is held here, and crowds along the Mall on that day can number half a million without too much of a problem (except when everyone tries to leave via the Smithsonian subway station at the end of the festivities).

Another annual event is a kite-flying competition held in late March or early April, when as many as 5,000 kites fill the air. Started by Paul Garber (see Paul E. Garber Facility under Maryland listings), it's a celebration of spring and childhood. Many of the contestants have long outgrown their childhood clothing, though. From box kites and newspaper kites to multilayered Mylar structures, it's a great day to be a kid again.

All competition kites must be made from scratch and they must fly at a minimum altitude of 100 feet for at least one minute. Awards are divided into several age groups. You can write to Margo Brown, 6636 Kirkley Avenue, McLean, Virginia 22101, for instructions on how to make some basic kites. Enclose a self-addressed, stamped envelope with two first-class stamps on it.

Jousting, Maryland's state sport, can be seen on the monument grounds usually during October.

☐ **Lincoln Memorial**

Memorial Circle between Constitution and Independence avenues. (202) 426-6841. Open daily 24 hours. Closed Christmas Day. Tourmobile stop. Smithsonian subway station.

The Lincoln Memorial is another special treat at nighttime. Looking from Lincoln's seat, you'll see the Reflecting Pool with the Washington Monument reflected in its waters. Only from Lincoln's eyes, it is said, can you see the entire Washington Monument reflected in the pool.

Because the memorial was built on swamp land, huge supporting pillars were set deep into the ground. The area between the pillars was not filled in and, in the brief 50 years of the memorial's existence, stalagmites and stalactites have formed. During the spring and fall, on Saturday and Sunday evenings, tours are given of this subterranean treasure, which includes cartoons supposedly drawn by the construction workers. The reservation procedure for this tour is cumbersome. You need to know which precise day and what precise hour to call. Find that out by calling (202) 426-6841, the same number to call for reservations. Then, on the appointed day, you must be willing to redial and redial and redial through the busy signal. Finally, you have to be flexible about which day you can take the tour. Not easy for locals; almost impossible for visitors.

Should you be fortunate enough to join a tour, bring a flashlight and a sweater (no matter how warm the day is), and wear comfortable shoes and slacks. The squeamish have a problem in here, so they shouldn't even think about it.

On the off chance some people decide against the tour, or never show up, ask a staff member what time the tour will start and if you can hang around to join it if there is space. The underground entrance is on the right side, as you're facing the memorial.

If you don't end up on a tour, enter the memorial on the left side (as you're facing it), as if to use the elevator, and look through the windows to see the superstructure. You will be able to catch a small glimpse of what you'd see on the tour. Although not perfect, this view is better than nothing, and it certainly sheds a new light on building construction.

☐ Vietnam Veterans Memorial

Constitution Avenue between Henry Balm Drive and 21st Street. (202) 485-9666. Open daily 24 hours. Tourmobile stop (Lincoln Memorial). Smithsonian subway station.

Two polished black granite walls set in a wide V form the board on which 58,132 names of dead and missing Vietnam veterans are inscribed. The veterans' names are carved alphabetically by the year each died, and a book, one at each end of the V, details on which panel each name can be found. Regardless of your feelings about this military action, this memorial, designed by Maya Ying Lin, is very moving. It is particularly poignant during a rainfall when the very granite seems to cry. People leave flowers, war medals, notes, pictures, and other items by the names of loved ones. These mementos are gathered regularly and catalogued in a collection that is not open to the public at this time.

A large selection of photographs and books that will help you explain and your youngster to understand the Vietnam conflict is available in the Lincoln Memorial gift shop.

☐ **Reflecting Pool**

Between the Washington Monument and the Lincoln Memorial.

The Reflecting Pool is home to ducks in the summer and ice skaters in the winter. Because the pool is fairly shallow, it can be secure with just a few days of subfreezing weather. National Park Service people will tell you if it's safe to skate.

☐ **Constitution Gardens**

Between the Washington Monument and the Lincoln Memorial. Open daily dawn to dusk. (202) 426-6841.

Commonly referred to as the Duck Pond, this 42-acre park contains a 6-acre lake, gardens, and an information center. A wooden bridge leads to a 1-acre island dedicated to the 56 signers of the Declaration of Independence. On the island stands a semicircle of knee-high granite stones that double as benches, and on each stone is inscribed the name, signature, hometown, and occupation of one of the signing fathers.

If you're planning to sit for a spell, go for one of the lesser names such as Josiah Bartlett (New Hampshire) or William Ellery (Rhode Island), rather than Hancock, Franklin, Adams, or Rodney. If you go for the biggies, you'll have to keep getting up because people always want to see the replicas of the most famous signatures.

The island and gardens are a nice place for sunbathing, biking, hiking, and for feeding the ducks and seagulls.

☐ **Tidal Basin**

15th Street and Ohio Drive (East Potomac Park). Open daily dawn to dusk. Tourmobile stop.

So named because it helps dissipate the incoming Potomac River tide, the Tidal Basin is the perfect place for looking at cherry blossoms and renting pedal boats. The Cherry Blossom Festival is held in late March or early April. In addition to the 1,233 Yoshing cherry trees growing around the Tidal Basin, which may or may not be in bloom during the festival, and the well-known parade, the festival is celebrated with a treasure hunt at the Constitution Gardens, band concerts, a pedal-boat regatta, and a ten-kilometer run. Even in the cherry blossoms there is a lesson for children to learn, for the Japanese compare the fleeting loveliness of the cherry blossoms (they may stay on the trees for as long as two weeks, but they may also last only three days) to the brevity of human life when compared to eternity, although both are wonderful and worthwhile. The Japanese have a saying for it: "Life is short, like the three-day glory of the cherry blossom."

Pedal boats (for two) rent for $5.15 per hour at the Tidal Basin boathouse, 15th Street and Maine Avenue, SW, from the end of March through the end of October, Wednesday through Sunday 10 A.M. to 6 P.M. They're contemplating augmenting the fleet with four-passenger boats and maybe even returning the swan boat so many old-timers remember.

☐ The Floral Library

Near the Tidal Basin, between the Washington Monument and Jefferson Memorial.

Created by the National Park Service in 1969, the living library opens its season in April with an incredible fanfare of tulips, and continues through the warm months with other flowering arrangements. Please feel free to walk between the beds, but don't pick the flowers and don't stand in the beds. Call (202) 619-7222 for more information about seasonal floral displays in the Washington area.

☐ Jefferson Memorial

South bank of Tidal Basin (14th Street and East Basin Drive, SW, East Potomac Park). (202) 426-6822. Open daily 24 hours. Closed Christmas Day. Tourmobile stop.

This famous site is perhaps best seen at dusk or nighttime, when it is bathed in floodlights. Dedicated to our third president, the memorial is programmed with short interpretive speeches, presented every half hour upon request. Children love to stand in front of the 19-foot statue of Jefferson, so have your camera ready to shoot the comparison.

☐ Hains Point

Hains Point, or East Potomac Park, is the peninsula created by the Washington Channel. Recreational activities abound here, as do beautiful views of the city. Automobile traffic sometimes is restricted, closely directed, or otherwise disturbed because of overcrowding.

The Awakening, however, is the main reason to visit Hains Point. Created by artist Seward Johnson, the sculpture is a half-buried body of a giant man emerging from the ground. Children particularly love to play with this big fellow, making a stop here another one of those terrific photo opportunities everyone raves about in Washington. There's talk about removing the statue and replacing it with a garden, so if you may not be back this way for another ten years, this is the time to visit.

The Tidal Basin is not the only place to view blooming trees when its cherry blossom time. East Potomac Park boasts more than 1,200 cherry trees, including Yoshing, Kawnzan, and weeping varieties. In all, there are some 3,000 cherry trees growing around the Tidal Basin, on the grounds of the Washington Monument, and in East Potomac Park.

☐ White House

1600 Pennsylvania Avenue. (202) 425-6975, (202) 456-1414. Open Tuesday through Saturday 10 A.M. to 12 noon, Saturday, during June, July, and August, until 2 P.M. Closed federal holidays and during special events. Guided tours are available. Tourmobile stop. McPherson Square subway station.

You can arrange for White House tours two ways. The first (and less desirable) way is to stop by the National Park Service booth on the Ellipse and pick up timed tour tickets. If you are visiting during the tourist season and do not have an early tour, you will have plenty of time to go off to do some other sightseeing and then return a little before your appointed time. This is not a narrated tour, but guides will answer questions. You'll see the Green Room (look for the Monet painting), the Blue Room (portraits of the first seven presidents), the Red Room (Gilbert Stuart's portrait of Dolley Madison), the great gold-and-white East Room (Gilbert Stuart's portrait of George Washington), and the State Dining Room (John Adams's blessing carved into the mantelpiece). The tour may last as little as ten minutes.

The second way is to write to your congressional representative (write early; there are relatively few tickets available) and ask for a VIP tour. This will allow you to enter the White House for an 8:30 A.M. tour that features real guides. In addition to the above-mentioned rooms, congressional tours see the lobby and three smaller rooms, the China Room, the Diplomatic Reception Room, and the Vermeil Room. Another advantage to this tour is that you're out early enough to do an entire day's sightseeing, or even make the early line at the Bureau of Engraving and Printing or the FBI Building.

A number of special events are held at the White House, such as the egg roll on Easter Monday morning for children eight and under. It takes place on the White House lawn and the eggs are provided. Children must be accompanied by an adult. The mid- to late-April Spring Garden Tours show off the beautiful gardens, including the Jacqueline Kennedy Rose Garden and the west lawn.

When the President leaves the city, he usually flies via helicopter to Andrews Air Force Base in nearby Prince George's County. The helicopters take off from the south lawn of the White House, so if you know this is scheduled (check the *Washington Post*), you can watch from the E Street area.

Stand on the Pennsylvania Avenue, or north side of the White House, around six o'clock on a busy news day and you're likely to see network television crews and White House reporters do segments for that evening's broadcasts.

The White House Christmas Candlelight Tour is available each season on two evenings only. This free tour, which begins at 6 P.M., is an opportunity to view the lovely White House Christmas decorations aglow with candlelight. Call (202) 456-2200 for information.

☐ Ellipse

During the last two weeks of December, the Ellipse grounds behind the White House are the site of the National Christmas Tree and nightly caroling, a Nativity scene, a burning yule log to warm chilled hands, and a glorious display of decorated Christmas trees, representing each state and territory in the United States. Call (202) 628-3400 for information.

A Twilight Tattoo is presented on the Ellipse by the U.S. Army Drill Team, the U.S. Army Band, and the Third U.S. Infantry (The Old Guard) with their Fife and Drum Corps every Wednesday at 8 P.M. from July 19 to August 30. The concerts are free and no tickets are required. Call (202) 475-0856 for information.

Behind the White House, on the Ellipse, is the zero mile marker. All mileage distances to Washington are measured from this spot.

Northwest Washington (including Downtown)

In this section, places of interest are listed by subway stations, and those not near a station are listed under the heading Elsewhere in the Northwest. Special sections are dedicated to the Georgetown and Dupont Circle areas, the latter of which is covered under the subway station of the same name.

Archives Subway Station

☐ **Canadian Embassy**

501 Pennsylvania Avenue. (202) 682-1740. Open Monday through Friday 10 A.M. to 5 P.M. Closed weekends. Archives subway station.

This is a newly built embassy and several rooms are open to the public, including a small art gallery featuring Canadian artists' works.

☐ **United States Navy Memorial Visitors Center**

Pennsylvania Avenue at Eighth Street. (800) 821-8892, (703) 524-0830. Open daily 10 A.M. to 5 P.M. Closed federal holidays. Archives subway station.

The center has an outdoor amphitheater that presents service bands and other performers, a commemorative area for official navy ceremonies, a world grid map (great for geography lessons) surrounded by bronze bas-relief sculptures depicting historical naval events, and the seven-foot-tall statue of the *Lone Sailor* gazing homeward from the far horizon. The *Lone Sailor* is the U.S. Navy bluejacket: young, maturing fast, enchanted by the seas and their beauty and strength. He's confident and believes in himself, his ship, his leaders, and his navy.

Inside the center is a wide-screen theater where works are shown that illustrate the importance of the seas to our nation. There also are exhibits, a reception area with a diorama, and navy artworks.

The Navy Memorial Log is a computerized roster of present and former navy members. It lists name, rank, date and place of birth, and dates of service alongside those of such naval heroes as John Paul

Jones, Stephen Decatur, Chester Nimitz, and William Halsey. Visitors will be able to display on a giant video screen individual names of family members, friends, or shipmates who are entered in the log. You can add a name and record for a $25 tax-deductible donation to the memorial.

A bookstore features gifts and commemorative items. During the summer, free concerts are performed by the various components of the U.S. Navy Band on Thursday evening at 8 P.M.

☐ **Washington Project for the Arts**

400 Seventh Street. (202) 347-8304. Open Tuesday, Wednesday, and Friday 10 A.M. to 5 P.M.; Saturday and Sunday 11 A.M. to 5 P.M.; Thursday 10 A.M. to 7 P.M. Closed Monday. No guided tours. Membership available. Archives subway station.

Elevated to hero status when it housed the controversial Mapplethorpe exhibit after the Corcoran Gallery cancelled it, this gallery specializes in showcasing Washington-area artists. Other attractions may be performance works and videos. To buy works from up-and-coming artists, attend the annual fall auction.

Cleveland Park Subway Station

☐ **National Zoological Park**

3000 block of Connecticut Avenue. (202) 357-2700 (Smithsonian informa-tion), (202) 673-4717 (direct line to zoo), (202) 357-1729 (TDD), (202) 357-1697 (voice recording). Buildings are open daily 9 A.M. to 6 P.M.; grounds are open daily 8 A.M. to 8 P.M. When going to the zoo, use the Cleveland Park subway station; it's downhill from the station to the zoo. When departing the zoo, use the Woodley Park/Zoo station; it's downhill from the zoo to the station. If you drive to the zoo and park in the lot, there is a $3 fee.

Thousands of animals, birds, reptiles, and many rare species, some of them gifts from foreign governments, fill this wonderful zoo. The Bird House has a free-flight room equipped with special temperature and humidity controls for its large collection of tropical birds, including fairy bluebirds, cock-of-the-rocks, and Rothschild's starlings.

The zoo's most famous residents are its two giant panda bears, Ling-Ling (female) and Hsing-Hsing (male), a gift to the children of America from the People's Republic of China. But there are also red panda bears, white tigers, and many other marvelous treasures.

The lions, tigers, and pandas are fed at 11 A.M. and 3 P.M.; the elephant demonstrations are at 11:30 A.M.. The Herplab, which is open

Wednesday through Sunday from 12 noon to 3 P.M., is where you can check out a box containing a live snake or frog and examine the reptile up close, put together a tortoiseshell puzzle, or see a movie about the zoo's lizards.

Sunset serenade concerts are presented from 6:30 to 8 P.M. every Thursday night during June and July on Lion/Tiger Hill. The repertoire ranges from jazz, bluegrass, and pop to folk, and the program may feature such local artists as John Lyon and his Gross National Product. No admission is charged; bring a picnic and a blanket. Call (202) 673-4717 for program information.

Volunteers of the Friends of the National Zoo (FONZ) conduct two-hour walking tours for groups of five or more from mid-March to May. To make reservations, call (202) 673-4955. Between April and the end of October, the zoo operates a train to take you to the Bird House, the Elephant House, and the cafeteria. The fee is nominal and the ticket is good for all day travel.

In front of the reptile house is a huge wooden sculpture entitled *Volunteers* that was carved from a single tree and is dedicated to the workers of FONZ. About 25 feet tall, the sculpture is filled with humans and animals, and it's a puzzle trying to figure out where and what everything is.

☐ Hillwood

4155 Linnean Avenue. (202) 686-5807. Two-hour guided tours are given daily, except Sunday and Tuesday, at 9 A.M., 10:30 A.M., 12 noon, and 1:30 P.M.; reservations are required. Spring and fall are extraordinarily busy times and reservations for these seasons must be made months in advance; March and November tours are much easier to arrange. Admission is $7 to the house and grounds, $2 to the American Indian exhibit and gardens only (11 A.M. to 3 P.M.). Children under 12 are not admitted. Reservations also are needed for tea. Closed January and February. The house is not wheelchair accessible.

During her four marriages and the rest of her life, Marjorie Merriweather Post compulsively accumulated things, particularly Russian and French decorative art pieces, and particularly when her second husband, Joseph E. Davies, was ambassador to the Soviet Union. Although she lived in this huge house with 40 rooms (but only three bedrooms), Hillwood was designed to be a museum for her extraordinary gatherings.

It's mind-numbing and even 12 year olds, the minimum age permitted entrance, may be too young to enjoy the experience, except for the exceptional child who's fascinated by collections of "things." It's almost too much for adults, and after hearing about the dozens of china place settings, and the multitudes of this and that, most people on the tour start asking questions about Post's daughter, Dina Merrill. The value of the collection probably is in the quantity gathered rather than in the quality, although the Russian imperial Easter eggs and other items by Fabergé are nothing to sneeze at.

The grounds, including rose gardens, a formal French garden, a Japanese garden, and the Friendship Walk dedicated to more than a hundred of Mrs. Post's friends, are gorgeous. The peak blooming times are when the azaleas, rhododendrons, and dogwoods are in bloom. From the south portico and the south lawn you can see across Rock Creek Park into downtown Washington.

Nearly 200 American Indian artifacts are displayed in the Indian Building. They include basketry, beadwork, leather moccasins, Navajo blankets, and pottery from the Hopi, Acoma, and Santa Clara tribes. The collection was moved here from Topridge, Mrs. Post's summer home in the Adirondacks. The building replicates the rough country nature of the camps constructed in upstate New York early in this century. Children seem particularly fascinated with the playing cards dating from the early 1900s made of tanned and painted hide. The suits are clubs, coins, cups, and swords, rather than the clubs, diamonds, hearts, and spades of today's cards. The display shows an Apache playing with the cards.

☐ United States Naval Observatory

Massachusetts Avenue at 34th Street. (202) 653-1543. Monday night celestial tours, with a look through the telescope, are at 8:30 P.M. in summer, 7:30 P.M. for late fall and early spring dates. Tours are held spring through fall only. Valid photo identification is required. Most appropriate for children over 12. Passes are issued to the first 100 people in line.

This, one of the most famous observatories in the world, is also the navy's oldest scientific institution. Established in 1844, it originally occupied a small office where chronometers, charts, and other navigational equipment were kept. It now encompasses a complex of 50 buildings on 72 acres of land.

Dupont Circle Subway Station

Dupont Circle is an environment unto itself. This is where the avant-gardist, the gay, the blue collar worker, and the executive merge to create one of Washington's most intriguing neighborhoods. On balmy summer nights, you'll find people virtually attached to the ten concrete chess tables on the south side of the circle until the wee hours of the morning. If you and your child have different chess abilities, each of you can find suitable level or challenging partners. At anytime there may be wandering minstrels. On Saturdays look for Joel Berg, who will write a poem for you for a couple of dollars.

Centered around Dupont Circle are seven museums and galleries, all members of the Dupont Kalorama Museums Consortium, which can be reached at (202) 387-2151. These include the Phillips Collection, the Textile Museum, the Woodrow Wilson House, the Anderson House, the Historical Society of Washington, the Meridian House International, and the Fondo del Sol Visual Arts Center. All but the Meridian House International are within a few blocks of the Dupont Circle subway station and of each other. The museums are located in elegantly restored mansions that have been homes to presidents and embassies. Call ahead for wheelchair accessibility.

Of the seven institutions, the Meridian House and the Phillips Collection are probably tuned into what interests younger children the most. The Textile Museum is suited to children who are at least ten years old. Other museums aim for junior-high or senior-high students.

The consortium presents a series of activities and tours throughout the year, including Walk Day (first Saturday in June with free admission), special art exhibits, music programs, demonstrations, and hands-on activities for all ages and interests. The first Thursday evening after Thanksgiving is Museum Shop Night, for those looking for unusual gifts. Free refreshments and transportation between the museums are provided.

☐ Anderson House Museum

2118 Massachusetts Avenue. (202) 785-2040. Open Tuesday through Saturday 1 to 4 P.M. Closed Sunday, Monday, and federal holidays. Self-guided or hour-long guided tours by appointment only. Dupont Circle subway station.

This is the headquarters, library, and museum of the Society of the Cincinnati, which was founded by General George Washington and the officers of the Continental Army in 1783. Exhibits pertain to the American Revolution and display such relics as the swords, firearms, and uniforms of the French regiments and the naval units that participated in the war. Military miniatures ready for battle and European and oriental decorative arts are on view. Most appropriate for older children or for any child who has studied the Revolutionary War.

☐ Columbia Historical Society

1307 New Hampshire Avenue. (202) 785-2068. Mansion is open Wednesday through Saturday from 12 noon to 4 P.M. Closed Sunday, Monday, Tuesday, and federal holidays. Hour-long docent-led tours of the mansion are con-

ducted throughout the day, with the last tour beginning at 3:15 P.M.; all
visitors to the house must join the tour. Adults, $2; senior citizens, $1;
children under 18, free. Library is open 10 A.M. to 4 P.M. Wednesday, Friday,
and Saturday. Washingtonian Bookstore and Victorian Garden are open
Tuesday through Saturday 10 A.M. to 4 P.M. Membership available. Dupont
Circle subway station.

Whatever it is you want to know about Washington—history, regional
and local trends, movements and personalities—you can find it at the
Columbia Historical Society, located in the Christian Heurich Mansion. The library houses 12,000 books, maps, and manuscripts, and
more than 70,000 photographs, 3,000 glass-plate negatives and lantern
slides, 1,500 etchings, many sketches and watercolors, and a complete
set of City Directories and major reference books related to the city.

The society offers museum tours designed for children, by appointment only, although it's best if the children already know something
about the city's history. Washington's domestic life since 1790, technology, Victorian architecture, and decorative arts are among the
subjects covered on the tour through this 31-room late-Victorian
mansion.

☐ Fondo del Sol Visual Arts Center

2112 R Street. (202) 483-2777. Open Tuesday through Saturday 12:30 to
5:30 P.M. Closed Sunday, Monday, and federal holidays. Admission is $1.
Self-guided tours, or guided tours by appointment only. Dupont Circle
subway station.

The center mounts changing exhibits of works by contemporary
artists who reflect the multicultural makeup of the Americas. There
are permanent collections of pre-Columbian art, santos (carved,
wooden saints), folk art, and contemporary art. Concerts, lectures,
poetry readings, performance art programs, touring exhibits, and
education programs are scheduled throughout the year.

An annual Caribbean Festival, held in late summer, features
outdoor performances of salsa and reggae music.

☐ Meridian House International

1624 and 1630 Crescent Place. (202) 667-6800. Open Tuesday through
Friday and Sunday 2 to 5 P.M. Closed Monday, Saturday, and federal
holidays.

Intercultural understanding is promoted here through changing
exhibits, lectures, and concerts. The two historic mansions housing
Meridian House were designed by John Russell Pope, one in classic
18th-century French style, the other in Georgian style. This is a
nonprofit educational and cultural institution that promotes interna-

tional understanding through a variety of conferences, services, and programs. A lively program of children's activities is available to acquaint youngsters with the multilingual, multiethnic community of Washington. The surrounding gardens offer a pleasant place to rest and reflect, and the view of Washington, from this perch on 16th Street at Crescent Place, is breathtaking.

☐ The Phillips Collection

1600 21st Street. (202) 387-0961 (recording), (202) 387-2151. Open Tuesday through Saturday 10 A.M. to 5 P.M., Sunday 2 to 7 P.M. Closed Monday and federal holidays. Free admission, but contributions are accepted. Tours are given on Wednesday and Saturday at 2 P.M.; lectures are given on the first and third Thursday of the month at 12:30 P.M. Tours for kindergarten through twelfth grade by appointment only. Museum shop is open Tuesday through Saturday 10 A.M. to 4:30 P.M., Sunday 2 to 6:30 P.M. Cafe hours are Tuesday through Saturday 10 A.M. to 4:15 P.M., Sunday 2 to 6:15 P.M. Sunday concerts and song recitals at 5 P.M. from September through May, except Easter; no reservations, so arrive early. Membership available. Dupont Circle (Q Street exit) subway station.

The Phillips Collection is the nation's oldest museum of modern art, featuring El Greco, Chardin, Manet, Bonnard, Braque, Cezanne, Klee, Monet, Rothko, O'Keeffe, and others. The collection is frequently rearranged, and special exhibits, concerts, lectures, and family programs are regularly scheduled.

The museum has an extensive children's program and a quarterly publication about parent-child workshops is available. You can ask to be placed on the mailing list.

"A Parent-Child Guide, A Child's Adventure into the Artists' World of Color," is a workbook for children 6 through 12 (voluntary contribution of 50 cents). It is designed for adults and children to use together, with sections for drawing and looking activities. A worksheet for high-school students called "Conversations with Art" involves a three-part critique, with each student choosing a painting and then writing about the way the artist used color, line, and subject matter in that painting to convey cultural history. Students then present their papers to the class.

☐ Woodrow Wilson House

2340 S Street. (202) 673-4034. Open Tuesday through Sunday 10 A.M. to 4 P.M. Closed Monday and federal holidays. Adults, $3.50; students and senior citizens (over 65), $2; children under 12, free. Guided tours are given throughout the day. Dupont Circle subway station.

School-class tours (from elementary on up) are given frequently and you may join them, which probably will give your children a more interesting perspective than the regularly available tour. Standard 45-minute tours follow a 30-minute film newsreel about Wilson's life and his fight for the League of Nations in Versailles. The tour also covers Mrs. Wilson's life as first lady and as private citizen. Children are particularly interested in objects from a life gone by, such as the Victrola with a wooden needle. Students who are old enough to have studied this period of history are the most appropriate age group for a visit.

President Wilson lived here after his presidency, until his death in 1924, and this is the only museum dedicated to a president in Washington.

☐ Textile Museum

2320 S Street. (202) 667-0441. Museum and museum shop are open Tuesday through Saturday 10 A.M. to 5 P.M., Sunday 1 to 5 P.M. Closed Monday and federal holidays. Free admission, but contributions are accepted. Walk-in highlights tours are given Wednesday and Sunday at 2 P.M. September through June. Library hours Wednesday through Friday 10 A.M. to 5 P.M., Saturday 10 A.M. to 2 P.M.

Serious studies of textiles take place here, but occasional exhibitions, such as ones that include Navajo rugs, probably would be interesting to children. Call about joining a school group for a specially tailored tour.

This is the place to learn everything you ever wanted to know about textiles, weaving, and related subjects. More than 14,000 textiles from around the world and 1,300 oriental carpets are housed here and the collection continues to grow. A library contains literature on all facets of textile art. Special exhibits, lectures, workshops, craft demonstrations, and seminars are given, and the gift shop is a treasure trove of handcrafted weavings, rugs, blankets, scarves, and other items.

☐ Kramerbooks & Afterwords Cafe

1517 Connecticut Avenue. (202) 387-1400. Open Sunday through Thursday 7:30 A.M. to 1 A.M., Friday and Saturday 24 hours. No cover charge, but a $3.95 minimum at the table. Dupont Circle subway station.

Kramerbooks is an institution around Dupont Circle, plus it's the obvious place to go when you want to buy a book in the middle of the night.

You can bring your older children to the cafe (in back of the bookstore) for an enjoyable evening of live music, from folk to jazz to blues. Try for a table upstairs or in the back (you can't hear the music in the atrium).

Farragut North Subway Station

☐ **Explorer's Hall, National Geographic Society**

17th and M streets. (202) 857-7588 (recording). Open Monday through Saturday and holidays 9 A.M. to 5 P.M., Sunday 10 A.M. to 5 P.M. Farragut North subway station.

Virtually everyone reads the *National Geographic,* and most children these days have been exposed to the little sibling of the yellow magazine, *National Geographic World.* Here they can live the discoveries and excitement of geography.

The south wing houses a number of different exhibits throughout the year, but the north wing is home to a permanent display, Geographica: A New Look at the World, that traditionally excites youngsters. They can touch a tornado, walk beneath a flying dinosaur, and play with interactive-computer displays that teach them about the earth. They can meet the world's peoples and study their customs; examine jungles, lonely mountain peaks, and the world beneath the sea; and look out to the moon, the planets, and the stars beyond. At the heart of Geographica is a 72-seat interactive amphitheater that allows visitors to explore a giant globe (11 feet in diameter and weighing 1,100 pounds). At their seats, "travelers" push electronic buttons to answer questions from a "pilot" narrator. Responses are analyzed by computer and displayed on twin video walls. It's all about the geography of the earth and the fragile balance that exists among its inhabitants, and it is presented in a way that children can visually and physically grasp. Evening lectures on a variety of topics are scheduled throughout the year.

☐ **B'nai B'rith Klutznick Museum and Exhibit Hall**

1640 Rhode Island Avenue. (202) 393-5284, ext. 203. Open Sunday through Friday 10 A.M. to 5 P.M. Closed Saturday and Jewish and federal holidays. Guided tours by appointment only. Farragut North subway station.

Ancient and modern Jewish ceremonial art objects, items of Jewish daily life, and an historic letter George Washington wrote to the Newport, Rhode Island, Hebrew congregation following a visit there are in the permanent collection. There are also changing exhibits of contemporary painting and sculpture organized along Judaic themes. An extensive library of Jewish Americana is available for research.

Farragut West Subway Station

☐ **Museum of Modern Art of Latin America**

201 18th Street. (202) 458-6019. Open Tuesday through Saturday 10 A.M. to 5 P.M. Hour-long tours are given on request, or by appointment. Farragut West subway station.

Rising behind the Pan American Union Building that houses the the Organization of American States, this structure was built by Andrew Carnegie in 1912. Blue tile and a terra-cotta fresco adorn the rear portico, which overlooks the lily pond in the Aztec Garden. The art here is diverse, collected from different Latin American countries, cultures, and traditions. Most appropriate for older children.

☐ **Daughters of the American Revolution (DAR) Museum and Constitution Hall**

1776 D Street. (202) 879-3239 (children's tour and children's program information), (202) 638-2661 (concert information), (202) 879-3254 (gift shop), (202) 879-3229 (library). Open Monday through Friday 9 A.M. to 4 P.M., Sunday 1 to 5 P.M. Hour-long tours are given Monday through Friday 10 A.M. to 3 P.M. (last tour starts at 2:15), Sunday 1 to 5 P.M. Children's tours (minimum second grade to take tour) are given Monday through Friday at 10:30 A.M. Farragut West subway station.

The property and headquarters of the Daughters of the American Revolution, the museum consists of 34 period rooms featuring decorative arts—furniture, ceramics, glass, paintings, silver, costumes, and textiles. The displays illustrate the artistry and craftsmanship of American artisans prior to the Industrial Revolution. Changing exhibits are presented in the museum gallery.

In the famed dollhouse exhibit, exceptional artisans decorated rooms to represent 28 states, revealing interesting tidbits about regional America. The doll collections and the schoolbooks used by pioneers children also are a favorite.

Constitution Hall, a 3,746-seat auditorium, presents concerts, lectures, and meetings, but the acoustics have been known to be terrible, so try for a seat on the floor near the front.

The DAR library, a genealogical research facility in the museum, is open Monday through Friday 9 A.M. to 4 P.M., Sunday 1 to 5 P.M.; closed to nonmembers in April. Nonmembers fee to use the library is $5 Monday through Friday, $2 between 11:30 A.M. and 1:30 P.M., and $3 on Sunday.

☐ **Old Executive Office Building**

17th Street and Pennsylvania Avenue. (202) 395-5895. Tours by advance reservation Saturday from 9 A.M. to 12 noon. Call for reservations Monday through Friday 9 A.M. to 12 noon. Security approval required; you must supply your social security number and birth date when making a reservation. Farragut West subway station.

This marvelous gingerbread house, with people for gargoyles, has interesting decorative items everywhere, even on the doorknobs (shield, anchor, and eagle reflecting the original history of this building, which housed the Departments of War, Navy, and State). The East Rotunda generally is the favorite area. Its centerpiece, designed by Richard von Ezdorf, is an oval skylight in blue, white, and salmon glass supported in the corners by sirens. Most appropriate for older children.

☐ **Department of the Interior Museum**

18th and C streets. (202) 208-4743. Open Monday through Friday 8 A.M. to 5 P.M. Closed federal holidays. Adults are required to show photo identification at the entrance. An Indian arts-and-crafts shop is open daily 8:30 A.M. to 4:30 P.M. (not affiliated with the department). Self-guided tours, or one-hour guided tours by appointment arranged at least two weeks in advance. Many school groups visit during the academic year, so call to see if you can join one of them. Farragut West subway station.

The Department of the Interior and the Bureau of Indian Affairs are the subjects of this museum. Children particularly like the dioramas showing historical vignettes, information about the westward expansion, and the displays of Indian objects, such as pottery, kachina dolls, stuffed eagles, and Indian headdresses. Perhaps the most unusual thing about the exhibits is that they show the warts as well as the beauty marks of the department. Another highlight is the display of murals created during the New Deal years.

Farragut West or Farragut North Subway Stations

☐ **Ansel Adams Collection**

900 17th Street, second floor. (202) 833-2300. Open Monday through Friday 10 A.M. to 5 P.M. Closed weekends and federal holidays. Farragut West (17th Street exit) or Farragut North (K Street exit) subway station.

This collection of about six dozen of the photographer's prints were selected by him, printed, and signed just before his death in 1984. It is the only major and permanent exhibit of his works on the East Coast. The photographs hang in the gallery of the Wilderness Society.

☐ Corcoran Gallery of Art

17th Street and New York Avenue. (202) 638-3211, (202) 638-1439 (recording). Open Tuesday through Sunday 10 A.M. to 4:30 P.M., Thursday until 9 P.M. Closed Monday and Christmas and New Year's days. Admission is charged for selected special exhibitions only. Tours of the permanent collection are offered Tuesday through Sunday at 12:30 P.M. and Thursday at 7:30 P.M. Membership available. Gift shop. Farragut West or Farragut North subway station.

The Corcoran has an extensive collection of American paintings, drawings, prints, and sculpture from the 18th century to the present. Its permanent displays include the William A. Clark Collection of European paintings and sculpture, tapestries, and pottery. The gallery also offers changing exhibits of prints by fine-arts photographers and regularly features the works of Washington-area artists.

The Musical Evening Series presents free chamber music concerts on Friday at 8:30 P.M., about once a month, between October and May. The renowned Tokyo String Quartet and Cleveland Quartet participate regularly in the series, performing on matched sets of Amati and Stradivarius string instruments owned by the gallery. Lectures, films, exhibition-related workshops, and special events are regularly offered.

☐ Renwick Gallery

17th Street and Pennsylvania Avenue. (202) 357-2700. Open daily 10 A.M. to 5:30 P.M. Closed Christmas Day. Guided highlights tours are given daily 10 A.M. to 1 P.M. Group tours should be arranged several weeks in advance by calling (202) 357-2531. Farragut West or Farragut North subway station.

Part of the Smithsonian Institution complex, but not located on the Mall, the Renwick showcases American design, crafts, and decorative arts, ranging from the chairs of Frank Lloyd Wright to the clocks of Wendell Castle. The building's Second Empire architecture and the Victorian-era paintings hanging in the elaborate Grand Salon belie the contemporary feel of most of the exhibitions. Comfortable sofas encourage a leisurely pace. Most appropriate for older children.

Federal Triangle Subway Station

☐ **National Theatre**

1321 Pennsylvania Avenue. (202) 628-6161 (ticket information), (202) 783-3372 (schedule for Saturday morning and Monday night children's programs). Federal Triangle subway station.

Pre-Broadway and touring companies fill the National's stage with topnotch entertainment. Children's programs featuring puppets, live music, dance, magic, vaudeville, and plays are presented Saturday morning at 9:30 a.m. on a first-come, first-seated basis. Doors open at 9:15 a.m. Activities for older children are scheduled for Monday night at 7 and at 8:30, also on a first-come, first-seated basis. Doors open at 6:45 p.m. Write to the theater's Outreach Program for a schedule; enclose a self-addressed, stamped envelope.

   Older, theatrically minded students can stop by the theater's fourth-floor archives to do research Monday through Friday 9:30 a.m. to 3:30 p.m. The archives collection, which was begun in 1976, houses 5,000 books, including reference works, biographies, and scholarly studies, plus scripts and sheet music. There is also a complete collection of National Theatre playbills dating to 1900, an architectural history of the National, and a poster from each production, signed by the performers, in the archives. If you have theatrical memorabilia in your attic or basement, call (202) 347-0365 and talk with archivist Tom Shorebird.

☐ **Freedom Plaza**

Across the street from the theater

Has a map of downtown Washington. The large letters carved into this granite park, between the National Theatre and the District Building, feature a paving design based on L'Enfant's 1791 plan for the city. Find Pennsylvania Avenue on the map and retrace the route you've traveled while sightseeing.

☐ **Shops at National Place**

Between 13th and 14th streets and E and F streets

Offers a variety of eateries and boutiques. Within the block are the J.W. Marriott Hotel, the National Theatre, The National Press Club, and the Washington bureaus of many distant papers and magazines.

☐ **Pavilion at the Old Post Office**

1100 Pennsylvania Avenue. (202) 289-4224, (202) 523-5691 (bell tower). Boutiques are open Monday through Saturday 10 a.m. to 8 p.m., eateries until 9:30 P.M.; Sunday 10 A.M. to 6 P.M. for stores and 12 noon to 6 P.M. for eateries. Tours of the bell tower are given daily 8 A.M. to 10:30 P.M. in summer, 10 A.M. to 5:30 P.M. in winter. The tower is closed the Fourth of July and Thanksgiving, Christmas, and New Year's days. Federal Triangle subway station.

The Old Post Office ain't what she used to be. Now there's a football-field-sized skylight over stores and boutiques, a food court, an entertainment stage, and a bell tower. Entertainment is provided just about every day at lunchtime, and "after work" in the early evening hours.

Tours of the bell tower are given by the National Park Service. The ten bells (which weigh more than 6 1/2 tons) were presented to the U.S. Congress by the British in honor of the bicentennial. The 20-minute tours start at the glass elevator and are conducted every 5 minutes for ten people (the elevator's capacity), but you may stay up in the belfry longer to take pictures. And this is a marvelous place for picture taking. You can see everything here that you can see from the Washington Monument, except for two things. You cannot see the shape of the Pentagon, and, of course, you cannot see the bell tower in the Old Post Office. The tower windows are large, wide, and extremely accessible. The tour explains change ringing, the art of ringing bells of various tones in various orderly progressions.

The carillon is played on Thursday from 7 to 9 P.M. when the Washington Ringing Society practices. Concerts are performed, usually around noon, on holidays and special events (no definitive schedule).

There are no tours of the bell tower when the ringers are practicing or performing, and the tower may also be closed due to weather conditions. Because Washington skies get yucky sometimes, it's best to go early in the morning, or when you can see the sky is crystal clear, particularly if you're planning to take pictures.

The National Park Service gives walking tours from the beginning of June through mid-October of the historic preservation project known as Pennsylvania Avenue. The one- to two-hour tour covers the avenue from the White House and the Treasury Building to the Capitol.

☐ Department of Commerce

14th Street and Constitution Avenue. (202) 377-2825 (recording). Open daily 9 A.M. to 5 P.M. Closed Christmas Day. Adults, $2; children 3 to 12 and senior citizens, 75 cents. Federal Triangle subway station.

There are three attractions of interest in this building. The first is the huge census clock in the lobby that ticks off the births, deaths, immigration, and emigration of literally everyone in the United States. It gives us an approximate total population count, second by second.

Although we most often hear about earthquakes in other parts of the country, the Washington area has been known to have a tremor or two, including one measured in Maryland in 1989. The second attraction, again in the lobby, is the seismograph machine that registers the vibrations of earthquakes.

The oldest aquarium in the country, the National Aquarium, is located on the lower level of the building. This institution can't hold a fishstick to the National Aquarium in Baltimore, but if you can't visit Charm City and the tanks at the National Museum of Natural History only whet your appetite, then this is the best game in town. Three nurse sharks and three lemon sharks (all babies between 20 and 48 inches long), octopuses, eyeless cave fish, lookdown fish, snapping turtles, sea anemones, baby alligators, and other strange and exotic species live here. There are no guided tours past the 70 tanks, but exhibits are well documented, and the helpful staff is always nearby (Room B-037) to answer questions. Piranha feeding is scheduled on Tuesday, Thursday, and Sunday at 2 P.M. Shark feeding is Monday, Wednesday, and Saturday at 2 P.M.

Spunky, the green sea turtle that began living here in 1969, moved in 1990 to the Clearwater Marine Science Center in Florida. At 46 pounds he outgrew his 3,000-gallon tank. He has been replaced by Dundee, a smaller Australian turtle.

Foggy Bottom/GWU Subway Station

☐ Albert Einstein Statue

2201 C Street. (202) 334-2000. Building is open Monday through Friday 8:30 A.M. to 5 P.M. Foggy Bottom/GWU subway station.

Children love to climb on Einstein's friendly lap, so this statue, located near the entrance to the National Academy of Sciences, is a perfect picture-taking spot. Good for picnics as well. Inside the academy are occasional art, photography, and scientific displays. There's also a Foucault pendulum. Top high-school students from across the country are selected by the Westinghouse Science Talent Search program and are honored in Washington every year. Their science projects are displayed here during the weekend they're in town, usually late February or early March.

☐ Department of State

2201 C Street. (202) 647-3241. Free one-hour tours of the eighth-floor diplomatic reception rooms are offered Monday through Friday at 9:30 A.M.,

*10:30 A.M., and 3 P.M.; reservations are required. Foggy Bottom/GWU
subway station.*

Part of the executive branch, this agency is responsible for formulating
and implementing U.S. foreign policy. The building also houses the
International Development Cooperative Agency, the Agency for
International Development, and the Arms Control and Disarmament
Agency.

Eighteenth-century English cut-glass chandeliers cast a warm glow
on the reception rooms that house 18th- and 19th-century decorative
arts, period furniture, and paintings. Corporations and private
citizens have donated most of the furnishings, with pieces by and in
the style of Chippendale, Hepplewhite, Queen Anne, Sheraton, and
Early American.

The secretary of state meets the press in the International Conference Room, while foreign dignitaries are received in the Diplomatic
Reception Rooms. A short, twice-weekly briefing is open to the public,
and is of particular interest to students studying government. Call
(202) 632-2406 for information or ask your congressional representative to make arrangements.

☐ **John F. Kennedy Center for the Performing Arts**
*New Hampshire Avenue at Rock Creek Parkway. (202) 467-4600, (800) 444-
1324 (recording about shows and ticket purchase), (202) 416-8341 (tours).
Hour-long tours are conducted daily 10 A.M. to 1 P.M., starting at the Motor
Lobby on parking level A. Tourmobile stop. Foggy Bottom/GWU subway
station.*

Tours, given by the Friends of the Kennedy Center, include the
theaters, lounges, and gifts from various countries. The famed seven-
foot-high Kennedy bust is in the Grand Foyer. The Hall of Nations
(between the Concert Hall and the Opera House) displays flags from
every country recognized by the United States, and the Hall of States
(between the Eisenhower Theatre and the Opera House) has a flag
from each state. Children enjoy finding their homestate flag or other
flags they recognize.

The Kennedy Center houses six theaters: the Eisenhower (usually
reserved for plays and comedies), the Opera House (musicals), the
Concert Hall (concerts), the Terrace Theater (small, intimate productions), the Theater Lab (for children's and experimental theater
productions), and the American Film Institute Theater (224-seat
auditorium for classic and new films). The Opera House and the
Eisenhower have audio loops for the hearing impaired. The Metropolitan Washington Ear provides an audio description for the visually
impaired during selected performances. For these audio-described

performances, they also will provide door-to-door transporation for the visually impaired who are in Prince George's, Montgomery, Arlington, Alexandria, and Fairfax counties, or within the District of Columbia. Call (301) 681-6636 for additional information.

Half-price tickets to Kennedy Center produced and presented attractions are available to students, persons with permanent disabilities, senior citizens, military personnel in grades E-1 through E-4, and others on fixed low incomes.

Theater for Young People stages music and theater of America and other countries for children from preschool on up. The show may present a fairy tale such as *The Billy Goat's Gruff*, the art of Kabuki, the music videos of Frank Cappelli, a kazoo band, a Trinidad and Tobago steel band, or the masks, costumes, music, and dances of a traditional Mexican-American festival. If you're a resident, or will be visiting frequently enough to order a season subscription, you can join the First Nighters' Club, which entitles you to three specific shows and a chance to talk with the actors and designers at the after-the-show parties. Shows are staged in the Theater Lab or the Terrace Theater.

A free Open House Arts Festival is held each year in late September from 12 noon to 6 P.M. More than 50 Washington-area artists present dance, music, and theater performances (including blues, classical, country, and gospel music; ballet, jazz, tap, ethnic, and modern dance; and puppets), with an emphasis on audience participation. Activities are held inside and outdoors.

Young people who will be in the area during July and August can apply for the Kennedy Center Theater for Young People, a component of the center's Education Department. An intensive four-week theater-training program is offered to 40 students, grades 5 through 12. They study performance and ensemble acting techniques, improvisation, character development, voice, and movement for the stage.

During the last three weeks of December, many free events are presented by local performers in the Grand Foyer. Weekend performances are every hour from 11 A.M. to 7 P.M. and weekday performances are held one hour prior to ticketed hall events.

One other place you should visit is the terrace that overlooks the Potomac and is in the flight path for planes landing at or departing from Washington National Airport. It can be a little noisy, but very pretty in the springtime.

Friendship Heights Subway Station

☐ **Washington Doll House and Toy Museum**

5236 44th Street. (202) 244-0024. Open Tuesday through Saturday 10 A.M. to 5 P.M.; Sunday 12 noon to 5 P.M. Closed Thanksgiving, Christmas, and New Year's days. Adults, $3; children under 14, $1. No admission charge to the gift shops. Friendship Heights subway station.

Grandparents will delight at the sight of toys and games they used to play with as children. Doll and dollhouse lovers will treasure this collection of antiques assembled by Flora Gill Jacobs, who started writing about and collecting the pieces in 1945. Under all this Victorian loveliness you will find that Mrs. Jacobs dedicated the museum to the proposition that antique dollhouses comprise a study of architecture and the decorative arts in miniature, and that toys of the past reflect social history.

Items displayed are but a small part of the collection, and special exhibits salute such annual occurrences as the baseball season, Easter, and Halloween. Among other exhibits was one that included miniature zoos, arks, and games of a zoological nature, which was lent to the National Zoological Park in 1978–9.

Children particularly like to ring the bell in the Ohio Schoolhouse belfry and to turn the handle on the W.S. Reed Capitol to see 1884 views of the Capitol and the White House roll past.

The Edwardian Tea Room with ice cream parlor tables and chairs is available for birthday parties. Two popular gift shops provide items for dollhouse collectors. One shop stocks miniature furniture, accessories, and dolls in what is considered one of the most complete inventories of its kind in the United States. The other shop is directed toward dollhouse builders, with a wide assortment of building and wiring supplies, kits, and books.

Gallery Place Subway Station

☐ **National Portrait Gallery** and **National Museum of American Art**

Eighth Street between F and G streets. (202) 357-2700. Open daily 10 A.M. to 5:30 P.M. Closed Christmas Day. These two galleries share one building. They also share a cafeteria open weekdays 10 to 11 A.M. for breakfast, and every day 11 A.M. to 3 P.M. for lunch. Walk-in tours (about 45 minutes) for the National Portrait Gallery are given weekdays 10 A.M. to 3 P.M., weekends at 11:15 A.M. Museum of American Art walk-in tours (about 45 minutes) are given weekdays at 12 noon and weekends at 2 P.M. Tours with sign language and oral interpreters (about 45 minutes) are available upon request (preferably with advance notice). School groups wishing to visit the Museum of American Art should call (202) 357-3095. Gallery Place subway station.

The National Museum of American Art is often referred to as the "unknown" museum, because its more frequently visited sisters in the Smithsonian family are all along the Mall and this one is a few blocks away. That generally means the crowds will be smaller and you will have more time to enjoy the displays.

The collection encompasses the full range of America's artistic ancestry, from colonial to contemporary, from masters to less-than-masters. Artworks carry the names of Gilbert Stuart, Mary Cassatt, John Singer Sargent, James McNeill Whistler, Winslow Homer, Robert Henri, and Helen Frankenthaler.

Occasionally, workbooks are created and family workshops are held to accompany a special exhibit.

One item in the permanent collection that simply fascinates people is James Hampton's *The Throne of the Third Heaven of the Nations' Millennium General Assembly.* The 177 glittering articles that make up the work are constructed of ordinary objects, such as bottles, old furniture, cardboard, kraft paper, desk blotters, transparent plastic, and light bulbs, all covered with aluminum and gold foil. A throne sits in the center, flanked by the Old Testament on the right and the New Testament on the left. Crowning the chair are the words "Fear Not," and tacked to Hampton's bulletin board is the inscription, "Where There is No Vision the People Perish." Although the work is religious in intention, most people tend to focus on the radiance, symmetry, decorative patterns, and eccentric improvisation of the throne. This is guaranteed to be one exhibit you'll never forget.

On the opposite side of the building are the National Portrait Gallery and the Archives of American Art. Together they house an extensive collection, including 250,000 paintings executed before 1914, 127,000 photographic negatives documenting works by more than 11,000 artists, and much, much more. An active program of lectures and seminars ensures that continuing research in the field is presented to a broad public.

A special collection in the museum consists of more than 1,400 diverse and dynamic works by black American artists. Among those people represented are Henry Ossawa Tanner, William H. Johnson, Palmer Hayden, Sargent Claude Johnson, William Edmondson, Eldzier Cortor, James Hampton, Jacob Lawrence, Bob Thompson, George W. White, Jr., Alma Thomas, and Sam Gilliam.

Another special collection showcases the huge family of Hispanic-American artists. The works range from the traditional religious painting and sculpture of José Benito Ortega and Pedro Antonio Fresquis (also known as the Truchas Master), the primitive carving of Patrocinio Barela, the folk sculpture of Felipe Archuleta, the painting of the self-taught artist Alexander Maldonado, and the drawings of the schizophrenic Martin Ramirez, to the more sophisticated modern work of Pedro Cervantez and Luis Jimenez.

☐ Hard Rock Cafe

999 E Street. (202) 737-7625. Restaurant and gift shop open daily 11 A.M. to 1 A.M.; after 9 P.M. gift shop can be entered only from inside the restaurant. Gallery Place subway station.

The cafe, as with others in the chain, is filled with memorabilia that the kids love (and enough "stuff" from our generation that we can be appreciative as well). Chubby Checker's checkered boots, the trumpet from Sergeant Pepper's Lonely Hearts Club Band, Elvis's hat and microphone, Al Jolson's Uncle Sam costume, and other items from or about Michael and Janet Jackson (uniforms), Grace Jones, Bo Diddley, Dion, Dave Edmonds, Wilt Chamberlain, and local celebrity Donna Rice.

The gift shop carries T-shirts, hats, watches, badge and guitar pins, key rings, towels, fanny packs, jackets, and other goods that are indispensable for HRC collections.

☐ Chinatown Friendship Archway

Seventh and H streets. Lit for an evening visit. Gallery Place metro.

This marvelously colorful arch marks the entrance to the eight-block Chinatown neighborhood, bounded by H, I, 6th, and 11th streets. Said to be the largest Chinese-motif archway in the world, the intricate red, blue, green, and gold foil structure has 7,000 tiles, 272 painted dragons in the styles of the Ming and Qing dynasties, and numerous other animals. The annual Chinese New Year's Parade of dancers, floats, and dragons passes under the arch. Several Chinese restaurants are located in the area.

☐ Techworld Plaza

800 K Street (Gallery Place or Metro Center subway station)

The largest privately owned mixed-use project in Washington. Three of its occupants that are of particular interest to children are Tech 2000, Holography World, and the Chinese Gardens.

☐ Tech 2000

Techworld Plaza, 800 K Street. (202) 842-0500. Open Tuesday through Sunday 11 A.M. to 5 P.M., Monday, 12 noon to 8 P.M. in summer; closed

Monday the rest of the year. Closed Thanksgiving, Christmas, and New Year's days. Adults, $4, children under 12, $3. Gallery Place or Metro Center subway station.

Computer buffs and computer phobics both adore this place and have been known to walk in when it opens at 11 A.M. and not depart until the doors close six hours later. It's easy to get involved. This is the land of interactive computers, the marriage of television and computers, and it comes with easy instructions. Children particularly like the home-entertainment area; others may prefer the research area. Computer phobics will delight in discovering how easy it is to conquer their phobia, plus they will enjoy learning about the extraordinary talents concealed in computers.

One favorite exhibit that has no keys for you to touch is Virtual Reality. You stand in front of a movie screen with a blue background behind you (it's the same way television programs use Chromakey to position weather forecasters in front of different maps and meterological patterns). You see yourself projected onto the huge screen and, by moving your hands and arms, you can select which subject you want to see and manipulate. Choose Music Video and your hand plays musical notes. Select Mystic Bubbles and you pop bubbles on the rise. With a third option, Word Game, you catch words and make sentences. No buttons to push, no computing to do.

Other computer setups will let you fly over Houston, ride down a bobsled run, view Andrew Wyeth's Helga portraits, or check out the video-disc system that holds 72 movies on one itty-bitty little disc.

☐ Holography World

Techworld Plaza, 800 K Street. (202) 408-1833. Open Tuesday through Saturday 10 A.M. to 6 P.M., Sunday 12 noon to 5 P.M. Closed Monday. Adults, $5; children under 12, $4. Gallery Place or Metro Center subway station.

Next door to Tech 2000 is the exhibit area for another wonder of the modern world, the Art, Science and Technology Institute—The Holography Collection. Exhibits include an international selection of holographic art pieces, including one of the world's largest holograms. See the computer chip through the microscope *in* the hologram. Look at the mountain range move back and forth, catch the kitten being playful, or see what a fire sprinkler looks like when it's sprinkling. They're amazing and some of them are for sale, probably starting in the several-thousand-dollar range. A guide accompanies you through the display of three-dimensional images to make sure you are seeing what you're supposed to be seeing.

Other works, certainly not of the caliber of those inside are posted around the outside of the gallery to help whet your appetite for what's inside. There is a gift shop that carries holographic calculators, watches, and other small items. The main offices of the institute are at 2018 R Street, NW; (202) 667-6322. Other holograms are displayed there.

Seminars and classes on holography are offered; they range from $26 per person to several hundred dollars for a long-term workshop.

☐ Chinese Gardens

The Chinese Gardens come last here, because you may need their tranquility after the extraordinary mental stimulation from the other two exhibits, and because the gardens represent a time and culture so apart from these modern scientific displays.

In an alcove off the pedestrian ways are three Chinese rock-and-tree gardens that were designed as "impressionistic sculpture." The gardens serve as quiet places of respite and inspiration for Techworld guests, and can be a nice eating place, with carry-out food shops conveniently located. These rocks, known as Taihu eroded limestone (*Taihu* means "great lake"), are from China, mined from the bottom of Jiangsu Province's Lake Tai.

Judiciary Square Subway Station

☐ National Building Museum

Judiciary Square, F Street between Fourth and Fifth streets. (202) 272-2448. Open Monday through Friday 10 A.M. to 4 P.M., weekends 12 noon to 4 P.M. Closed Thanksgiving, Christmas, and New Year's days. Guided tours are given Monday through Friday at 12:30 P.M., Saturday, Sunday, and federal holidays at 1 P.M.; reservations are required. Some exhibits are more interesting to children than others; call for a schedule. Membership available. Judiciary Square (F Street exit) subway station.

One permanent highlight of this monument to the building arts in America is an exterior terra-cotta frieze that encircles (1,200 feet long, 3 feet high) the building and depicts a processional of veterans returning from the nation's wars. It is dedicated to all who gave their lives for an ideal.

This museum is devoted to the study of architecture and how it reflects and affects our lives. At one time this structure was the Pension Building and one of the permanent exhibits, which includes an audiovisual program, is about the building's history. Another exhibit looks at the Brooklyn Bridge, with seven full-scale, three-dimensional models explaining the unique construction. Try doing that with an Erector Set.

It has been said that the steps in this 1880s building were constructed with unusually short risers so horses could more easily walk up them to their quarters on the top floor, where plenty of air circulated through the windows. Museum officials denounce this tale as rumor and hearsay. But whom are you going to believe? A group of experts or a good story about horses?

McPherson Square Subway Station

☐ Bethune Museum and Archives

1318 Vermont Avenue. (202) 332-1233. Open Monday through Friday 10 A.M. to 4:30 P.M., Saturday and Sunday by appointment. Hour-long tours are available by appointment. Adults, $1; children under 15, 75 cents. Membership available. McPherson Square subway station.

This Logan Circle Victorian townhouse was the former home of civil rights leader and educator Mary McLeod Bethune. Today it provides a backdrop for changing and permanent art and history exhibits that focus on African-American women's issues.

☐ Washington Post

1150 15th Street. (202) 334-7969. Guided one-hour tours are given Monday and Thursday at 10 A.M., 11 A.M., 1 P.M., and 2 P.M.; reservations are required and children must be at least 11 or in the fifth grade. McPherson Square subway station.

Children watch newspaper operations so much on television, from the old mom-and-pop paper to the big-city newsroom, that you'd think there's nothing new to see. A visit to the *Post* changes that opinion, because there's no way to appreciate how many people are involved and how much activity goes into the paper's production until you see it in person.

The tour takes you to the newsroom, production area, and the press room, although the presses are not running during the visit (the *Post*, a morning paper, is printed at night).

Metro Center Subway Station

☐ National Museum of Women in the Arts

1250 New York Avenue. (202) 783-5000. Open Monday through Saturday 10 A.M. to 5 P.M., Sunday 12 noon to 5 P.M. Tour programs in development stage; call for information. Metro Center (13th Street exit) subway station.

This is one of the newest museums in the city, and the only one dedicated to women's historical contributions to art. It's docent and tour programs are still being developed and expanded. Special tours for families with children usually are conducted on Sunday afternoon, and reservations are requested. Guided walk-in tours usually are given twice a day, depending on docent availability. Guided reserved tours ($5 per person) need advance request notice.

Although most children tend to prefer the contemporary art in this collection, they all seem to love the building, starting from when they walk in and see the huge, lovely open-space lobby with winding marble staircases on either side of the Great Hall.

There are numerous changing and permanent exhibits, and the Education Department is working toward a family activities guide for the both permanent collection and for the major temporary exhibits.

☐ Federal Bureau of Investigation

Ninth Street and Pennsylvania Avenue. (202) 324-3447. Open Monday through Friday 8:45 A.M. to 4:15 P.M. Closed federal holidays. Cameras are not allowed. Metro Center subway station.

Also known as the J. Edgar Hoover Building, this stop offers one of the more popular tours in town. "Everyone" knows you get to see all kinds of guns, an agent practicing in the basement firing range, posters of the "ten most wanted criminals," mini spy cameras, hollowed-out coins that hide microdots, a walking cane that is actually a shotgun, and other representations of the "bad guys" of drugs, terrorism, organized crime, bank robbery, and white-collar crime versus the "good guys."

Arrive early to avoid the up-to-two-hour lines (in peak tourist season) or write to your congressional representative for FBI tour passes that are scheduled for a specific time. This tour is not recommended for children under seven, not because of what it shows, but because youngsters that age normally aren't tall enough to see through the glass windows.

The hour-long tour starts every 15 or 20 minutes. It takes visitors past (separated by glass windows) laboratories, (serology, ballistics and microscopic analysis, fingerprint files), an array of about 5,000 plus guns, 80 percent of which were confiscated or donated (mostly from criminals); and the room where the FBI displays $1.5 million worth of jewelry and furs confiscated from drug dealers. Along the way, you'll see G-Man toys from the 1930s and 1940s, and a safety film done by Bill Cosby. You will end up at the range for target practice, a stop that may include a few dozen hollow-tip .38-caliber, 9mm, and machine-gun slugs fired at the heart of a paper-target bad guy. A question-and-answer session follows with the agent from the firing demonstration.

A noontime Courtyard Concert Series is scheduled periodically from May to September, usually featuring military bands.

☐ Ford's Theatre/Lincoln Museum

511 Tenth Street. (202) 638-2941 (ticket information), (202) 426-6924 (museum). Open daily 9 A.M. to 5 P.M. Closed Christmas Day; theater is closed for matinees and rehearsals. No guided tours. The museum is not wheelchair accessible. Metro Center (11th Street exit) subway station.

Restored in 1968, Ford's Theatre, where President Abraham Lincoln was fatally shot on April 14, 1865, has been restored once again. The presidential box, where Lincoln was sitting during a performance of *Our American Cousin*, is as it was. The basement houses a museum of objects used by Lincoln in his personal and public life, as well as exhibits about the assassination plot. Clothing, the assassin's gun, photographs, editorial cartoons, and other memorabilia almost give life to this tall man. And if you want to see how tall he was, compare yourself with the Measure of Lincoln.

The restoration of the theater as a museum and a performing-arts venue can be attributed to the hard work and dedication of such people as executive producer Frankie Hewitt and Ford's Theatre Board of Trustees member Roger Mudd (whose relative was accused of being part of the plot because he set Booth's broken ankle, and then was later exonerated).

Regular theatrical productions are presented here, almost all of which are suitable for family audiences.

☐ Petersen House

526 Tenth Street. (202) 426-6830. Open daily from 9 A.M. to 5 P.M. Closed Christmas Day. No guided tours. The house is not wheelchair accessible. Metro Center (11th Street exit) subway station.

Across the street from Ford's Theatre is the home where the dying President Lincoln was carried. Mary Todd Lincoln and her son Robert spent the night of April 14 in the front parlor, the first room to the left. Through the double doors is the back parlor, and in the rear of the house at the end of the hall is where Lincoln died. The rooms are decorated much as they were on the night of the assassination. The furnishings are not original, but they are either good reproductions or pieces from the same period. Look at the bed and realize that Lincoln was much taller than it was long.

☐ **Treasury Building**

Pennsylvania Avenue and 15th Street. (202) 343-9136 (recording of open tour dates). Tours are given alternate Saturdays at 10, 10:20, and 10:40 A.M.; reservations are required at least three days in advance, and you must provide the name, birth date, and social security number of everyone who will attend. Adults need a photo identification upon arrival. Video cameras are not allowed. Enter on the lower level (marked Employees Entrance) on the 15th Street side. Metro Center or McPherson Square subway station.

Blocking the view from the White House to the Capitol, this building is noted for its balconied marble hall (72 by 32 feet and 27 1/2 feet high), an 1864 burglarproof vault, and the suite of rooms that once served Andrew Johnson as a temporary White House. Wear flat shoes for there are lots of steps.

☐ **TICKETplace**

F Street Plaza between 12th and 13th streets. (202) TIC-KETS (842-5387) (recording). Open Tuesday through Friday 12 noon to 4 P.M., Saturday 11 A.M. to 5 P.M. Half-price tickets for Sunday and Monday shows, if available, are sold on Saturday. Metro Center (12th Street exit) subway station.

This is the place to go for half-price, day-of-performance tickets for dance, music, and theater to such well-known Washington-area venues as Arena Stage; Kennedy Center; Lisner Auditorium; Washington Project for the Arts; Dance Place; the Folger, Ford's, Hartke, National, and Warner theaters, and a variety of dinner and alternative theaters. They also handle advance-purchase full-price tickets. This is a cash-only operation. A service charge of 10 percent of the full-price value is levied on each half-price ticket; full-price tickets carry a $1 service charge. Performance availability is posted on a board outside TICKETplace, or you can tune to WGMS (103.5 FM) Saturday at 10:05 A.M. for a listing.

Elsewhere in the Northwest

☐ **London Brass Rubbing Centre**

4954 MacArthur Boulevard. (301) 279-7046. Open Tuesday through Sunday 10 A.M. to 4 P.M. Closed Monday.

The center has medieval knights and ladies, kings and merchants in brass for visitors to use in making their own pictures of these historical figures. All materials are provided and you can end up with some beautiful wall hangings. A small fee (about $3) is charged.

A picture is made by rubbing a piece of beeswax in short, up-and-down strokes over white or black rag paper that is stretched over a raised brass figure. Then you polish the rubbing with a cloth until it shines. Children can finish in about 15 minutes.

☐ **Rock Creek Park**

Tilden Street and Beach Drive. (202) 426-6832. Sections of Beach Drive are restricted to bicycle riders and other nonmotorized traffic from 7 A.M. Saturday morning until 7 P.M. Sunday evening, extended through 7 P.M. Monday if it is a federal holiday.

Whatever you might wish to do in a park, you probably can do here. There's hiking, biking, horseback riding, police canine demonstrations, an art barn, an old mill, a golf course, an orienteering course, tennis courts, picnic areas (some need reservations), a planetarium, a nature center, and more. Of course, the National Zoological Park is located in the park as well. Information on some of these attractions follows.

☐ **Art Barn Gallery**

Rock Creek Park, 2401 Tilden Street. (202) 244-2482. Open Wednesday through Saturday 10 A.M. to 5 P.M., Sunday 12 noon to 5 P.M. Closed Monday, Tuesday, and federal holidays. Tours are given Wednesday, Thursday, and Friday at 10 A.M., 1 P.M., and 3:30 P.M.; reservations are suggested.

Local professional artists display their works here in rotating exhibits throughout the year. Art classes are offered on Saturday morning with a different artist-in-residence each month. Artist demonstrations are held on Sunday from 1 P.M. to 3 P.M.

☐ **Peirce Mill**

Rock Creek Park, Beach Drive and Tilden Street. (202) 426-6908. Open daily 10 A.M. to 3:30 P.M. Closed federal holidays.

The last of eight 19th-century flour mills along Rock Creek, the Peirce Mill is an authentic restoration of an 1820 grist mill. Costumed helpers grind grain into flour, which is then sold for about $2 to $4 per pound. Choices may include buckwheat, corn, rye, or other flours, depending upon what's in stock. You can watch demonstrations of butter churning and batter-cake making, tour art exhibits, or participate in a children's activity day. You also may encounter lacemaking, stone carving, dulcimer making, fish-decoy carving, wheat weaving, and basketmaking demonstrations.

☐ Rock Creek Nature Center

5200 Glover Road. (202) 426-6828. Open daily 9 A.M. to 5 P.M. Closed federal holidays.

The buildings and nature trails are designed to teach youngsters about the natural world and their relationship to it. An exhibit hall displays examples of local animal life, including a live bee colony, and minerals. The nature walks, led by park rangers and scientists, usually emphasize a single theme—ecology, mushrooms, Indian life. They are given weekdays to accommodate school groups, but weekend tours also are available.

The center includes a planetarium that presents two free shows, at 1 and 4 P.M. on Saturday and Sunday. The early show, An Introduction to the Night Sky, is for ages four and up; the four o'clock show is geared to children seven and up and changes monthly. Free tickets are handed out 30 minutes before each show.

☐ Washington National Cathedral

Officially the Cathedral Church of St. Peter and St. Paul, Massachusetts and Wisconsin avenues, at Woodley Road. (202) 364-6616 (recording), (202) 537-6200, (202) 537-8982 (herb cottage), (202) 537-6263 (greenhouse). Open daily 10 A.M. to 4:30 P.M., until 9 P.M. in summer. Walk-in tours are given Monday through Saturday 10 A.M. to 3:15 P.M., Sunday at 1 P.M. and 2 P.M., hours subject to change. Special-interest tours and a Tuesday tour that includes a tea break (charge) are available; call (202) 537-6207. Observation Gallery is open Monday through Saturday 10 A.M. to 3:15 P.M., Sunday 12:30 P.M. to 3:45 P.M. Membership available. Tourmobile stop.

After 83 years of on-again, off-again construction (an amazingly short amount of time for an undertaking of this size), this Gothic cathedral had its last stone set and was formally consecrated in September 1990.

For a self-guided tour of the cathedral, pick up the turquoise-colored brochure near the entrance. A free 30-minute tour starts by the Space Window, a stained-glass creation dedicated to the Apollo 11 moon landing. In the center of the window is a piece of moon rock. At this point, any child who is old enough to think a cathedral tour might be really dull snaps to attention.

The Children's Chapel, built to a child's scale, is interesting, as is the War Memorial Chapel with its image of the raising of the flag at Iwo Jima worked into the lower left-hand corner of the stained-glass window. There's also a Maryland window, and several pieces of glass form prisms that cast rainbows of colors onto the floor and the people passing under their rays. Flags of the 50 states are located along the nave, and a prayer is said for one state each week.

The Observation Gallery (push the seventh floor button in the elevator) has a short film about the construction and history of the cathedral and offers some pretty spectacular views from the 70 windows overlooking all of the Potomac Valley, including Tysons Corner in Virginia and the faraway Blue Ridge Mountains. Other views from the gallery include the cathedral's buttresses, towers, and a limited look at some of the gargoyles. You can see the 103 gargoyles and grotesques in more detail if you bring field glasses (it's said that only God and the pigeons see the tops of the gargoyles). The construction display shows a couple of miniature examples, including a grotesque shaped like a television cameraman in honor of the numerous Christmas masses and other services broadcast from the cathedral. The gargoyles and grotesques are used in the rain drainage system; the gargoyles have water spouts but the grotesques do not. A television documentary about the stone carvers and their carvings won an Emmy Award.

Another pretty good view is from the south lawn, where the Peace Cross stands.

Although the cathedral is 676 feet above sea level, the bell tower itself is only 301 feet tall. Thus, the Washington Monument is a taller building even though the cathedral is 60 feet higher. The 53-bell carillon weighing 60 tons is played weekdays from 12:15 to 12:45 P.M. A 10-bell ring, the only one of its kind in the world, is rung following the 11 o'clock service every Sunday. The carillon is played on Saturdays at 5 P.M. (12:30 P.M. in winter). Visitors are not permitted to the top of the bell tower.

The cathedral has a Medieval Workshop that is a hands-on activity center where families can learn something about the crafts that go into the building of a Gothic cathedral. You can piece together a stained-glass window, build stone arches as a mason (learning a little physics lesson along the way), lay a flagstone patio, try your skill as a stone carver, discover the artistry of the blacksmith, create a piece of needlework, and design your own gargoyle or grotesque. *National Geographic World* magazine sponsored a design contest for children and the winning entries, on display here, were carved by the cathedral's mason and then mounted. Among them is one called the Sagacious Grotesque, who holds an umbrella up to protect itself from the rain. The workshop is open Saturdays from 11 A.M. to 2 P.M. and there's no charge. Admission is on a first-come, first-served basis, but try to tour the cathedral first. The workshop is closed during August. Call (202) 637-2930 for information.

Other attractions are the herb cottage (you can purchase dried herbs for flavor or scent), a greenhouse, and a gift shop. State guest books are available for you to sign in as a visitor of the cathedral. During the school year, organ demonstrations are held on Wednesday at 12:15 P.M. and the walls virtually shake when the 11,500 pipe organ is played. Sunday afternoon organ recitals following evensong are scheduled, performed by visiting organists.

Georgetown

Georgetown, named in honor of King George II, started as an Indian trading center in the 1600s and was a busy tobacco port by the later half of the 18th century. Now it's an eclectic mix of smart boutiques, intriguing bookstores, pricy restaurants, and outdoor cafes (weather permitting). It's a great place for "cruising" to see the local sights and personalities and for "cruising" along the canal. Some eateries have been here for decades; others seem to appear and disappear over-night. Fast food also is available.

Parking can be difficult and your pocket can be picked, so watch the parking prohibition signs (particularly on weekends and on neighborhood streets) and be careful when you're walking and shopping.

☐ C & O Canal Barge Rides

Foundry Mall, 1055 Thomas Jefferson Street (ticket office). (202) 472-4376 (recording), (202) 653-5844. Hours and days vary; summer barge trips depart Wednesday through Sunday at 10:30 A.M., 1 P.M., and 3 P.M.; reduced schedule in effect in spring and fall. Adults, $4; senior citizens (62 and over), $3; children 12 and under, $2.50.

You can explore the area via mule-drawn canal rides, at Georgetown in Washington and at Great Falls in Potomac, Maryland, from about mid-April through mid-October. Conducted by the Georgetown C & O Canal National Historical Park, the rides re-create what life was like on the barges more than a century ago.

The 90-minute round trip aboard the *Georgetown* takes you through the historic part of town. Guides wear period costumes and warn you against asking questions about things that happened after 1876, because theoretically this ride takes place then. (They will, of course, answer any serious questions about the canal, which operated from about 1830 to 1924, and related subjects that occurred after that year.) The 90-foot boat is moved through a lock process that visually explains how boats are lifted and lowered from one water level to another.

One-hour day trips and two-hour evening trips can be booked by groups, at special rates. Bring along a banjo or guitar and have an old-fashioned sing-along.

☐ Dumbarton Oaks

1703 32nd Street. (202) 342-3200, (202) 342-3212 (recording, except on Thursday mornings between 10 A.M. and 12 noon when a real person is available to talk with you). Museum is open Tuesday through Sunday 2 to 5 P.M. Museum is closed Monday and federal holidays. Free admission, but a $1 contribution is suggested. Group tours of the museum are given Tuesday, Wednesday, Thursday, and Saturday; reservations are required. Ten acres of formal gardens are open daily 2 to 6 P.M. from April 1 to October 30, 2 to 5 P.M. from November 1 to March 31. Gardens are closed on federal holidays. Admission to the gardens is adults, $2; children under 14, $1; senior citizens, free on Wednesday.

The museum contains two impressive collections, one of pre-Columbian art and one of Byzantine art that includes a library of more than 80,000 volumes. Younger children (eight and older) should enjoy the pre-Columbian displays of sculpture and gold, but most of the museum's exhibits are more appropriate for older children. Many garden enthusiasts consider these gardens among the most enchanting in the country.

☐ Old Stone House

3051 M street. (202) 426-6851. Open Wednesday through Sunday 8 A.M. to 4:30 P.M. Closed Monday, Tuesday, and federal holidays. Limited wheelchair accessibility.

This is one of the first dwellings built in Washington and the oldest in Georgetown. It was constructed in 1765 and is considered an excellent example of pre-revolutionary architecture. Colonial-costumed guides take visitors through the house and demonstrate early American cookery, spinning, weaving, candle dipping, and pomander making. Children particularly enjoy the craft demonstrations, and special children's days are scheduled periodically, with the entire day focused on family activities. The National Park Service has restored this house and maintains its colorful gardens.

☐ **Tudor Place**

1644 31st Street. (202) 965-0400. Open Tuesday through Saturday by appointment only. Tours at 10 A.M., 11:30 A.M., 1 P.M., and 2:30 P.M.

Tudor Place is an historic house and garden. For two centuries the neoclassical mansion, filled with family collections, was occupied by the Custis-Peters, descendants of Martha Washington. A children's program is in the works.

☐ **Hamburger Hamlet**

3125 M Street. (202) 965-6970. Open Sunday through Thursday 11 A.M. to 12 midnight, Friday and Saturday until 1 A.M.

Besides offering a nice hamburger and a quick lunch, HH has crayons tableside and white drawing paper on the tabletops to encourage big and little artists to color their own placemats. The good ones go up on the wall, and you'll find masterpieces from the famous and the not-yet-famous. In the back room, on the right, is a framed Conehead drawing by Dan Aykroyd.

Southwest Washington

☐ Arena Stage

Sixth Street and Maine Avenue. (202) 554-9066 (administrative office), (202) 488-3300 (box office). Waterfront subway station (opening late 1991).

Arena, Washington's most prestigious resident theater company (started in 1950 by Zelda Fichandler), actually houses three theaters, the 827-seat Arena (a theater in the round), the smaller 500-seat Kreeger, and the intimate 180-seat Old Vat Room. Almost any play presented here will be appropriate for children as far as language is concerned, but the subject matter of some plays may be suitable only for older children. Check with the administrative office if you have any concerns.

☐ Maine Avenue Fish Market

Maine Avenue and Eighth Street. Open daylight hours.

Tucked along the waterfront, under the expressway flyovers, are seafood markets where you can find fresh fish, local and imported, as well as seasonal produce. If you've never seen bushel baskets mountained over with live Chesapeake Bay blue crabs, squid, stone crab claws, octopuses, shrimp, salmon, perch, trout, catfish, or any number of other fish types, this is the place to visit. It's also the place to buy fresh produce.

The boats, which double as stores, are in the water; you stand on the land and the transactions are handled over ice shavings and all that fresh fish. If you're squeamish about cleaning the fish, take them into Ben Edwards's fish-cleaning house and watch the guys adroitly use electric scalers and a variety of knives to set those fish in proper order.

☐ Postal Service

475 L'Enfant Plaza. (202) 268-2000. Open Monday through Saturday 9 A.M. to 5 P.M. Closed Sunday and federal holidays. No guided tours. L'Enfant Plaza subway station.

The Philatelic Sales and Exhibition Room tells the story of our mail system and includes many little-known facts in the tale. One such historical footnote is that George Washington wrote the first letter to travel by air (balloon) on January 9, 1793; it was flown from Philadelphia to Deptford, New Jersey. Display cases show commemorative, historic, and current United States stamps and a good number of foreign ones, many of which are for sale.

☐ **Voice of America**

330 Independence Avenue. Visitors must join a guided tour. Tour entrance is between Third and Fourth streets on C Street, in the middle of the building, marked with a blue- and-white sign reading VOA. Tours, lasting about 35 minutes, are by appointment only Monday through Friday at 8:40, 9:40, and 10:40 A.M., and at 1:40 and 2:40 P.M. Call Barbara Jaffie at (202) 619-3919 for tour information. Closed weekends and on federal holidays. Federal Center SW subway station.

Because so many television sports and news programs have a camera in a control room, or a newsroom, most children already know what a working television or radio station looks like. What makes the Voice of America (VOA) different is its mission, which is to broadcast 1,200 hours of news, music, and commentary every week to more than 100 countries with a weekly audience of 130 million people. Yes, there are only 168 hours in a week, but VOA broadcasts in 42 languages and the 1,200 hours include all the time when someone is broadcasting.

Starting in the lobby, you view a short videotape on the history of VOA, which has been in operation since 1942, and how it works. Then it's a visit past the control room, the newsroom (which has a bunch of desks, computer terminals, and people rushing around), the studios, and the "bubble." Outside the studio, you can twist a button to hear the language of the radio show being aired, which might be anything from Russian to Romanian. The "bubble" is where telephoned reports from all the correspondents overseas are received. These will be translated or aired as they are. On the walls are exhibits about the history of VOA, and there is an old master control room from before the days of computers.

Southeast Washington

☐ **Frederick Douglass National Historic Site**

1411 W Street. (202) 426-5960. Open daily 9 A.M. to 5 P.M. from April to October, 9 A.M. until 4 P.M. the rest of the year. Closed Christmas and New Year's days. Free admission, but contributions are accepted. Candlelight tours, starting about dusk and with guides in period costumes, are available periodically (call for dates); reservations are required for a group of ten or more. Tourmobile stop.

Ideally, your visit to the Frederick Douglass home will start at the visitor center, where you can watch a film about his life. There are two movies, one is 17 minutes long and usually shown to students. The other is 33 minutes long. These are not award-winning flicks and suffer in comparison to the high-tech laser-light, rap-song entertainments our children are exposed to daily. The movies explain Douglass's life and define the context in which he, Harriet Tubman, and John Brown lived and worked. The movie is scheduled to start every hour on the hour.

If you arrive just prior to the half hour, you'll be taken on a tour of the house first (it's a locked-door tour and the entire group of no more than 22 people must stay together) to see the sitting rooms, bedrooms, kitchen, and other areas.

Most of the objects in the house are original to Douglass, the famed 19th-century abolitionist, editor, and African-American leader, and a visit is a great way to introduce children to someone they read about in history books. Douglass was born the son of a slave and never formally educated, yet he became a commanding influence in America's battle for equal rights. There's a good lesson in how important it is to learn to read and write. For those who have seen the movie *Glory,* Douglass had two sons fight in the storming of Fort Wagner, and a picture of the black military unit hangs on the wall. The large home is typical of upper-middle-class white or African-American homes in the late 19th century. When school-groups tour, the National Park Service guides provide more of a treasure-hunt format, such as seeing if students can find the wheelchair, the chamber pots, and so on. You can call for a schedule of upcoming class tours and join one of them.

From the west lawn, about halfway up the steps, you can see a pretty good view of Washington, including the Capitol, the John F. Kennedy Center for the Performing Arts, and the Shrine of the Immaculate Conception. The view is better when the trees are naked, however.

The visitor center is fully accessible to the handicapped, and there is a driveway up to the house that can be used as a ramp. The house has steps and is not accessible. A gift area, with plenty of books by and on Douglass and related matters, is located in the center.

☐ Anacostia Neighborhood Museum

1901 Fort Place. (202) 287-3369. Open daily 10 A.M. to 5 P.M. Closed Christmas Day. Guided tours of 45 to 60 minutes are given Monday through Friday at 10 A.M., 11 A.M., and 1 P.M. (202) 287-3369.

African-American culture and history is featured in changing exhibits with a program of lectures, workshops, films, and performing arts related to each exhibit. The museum is dark for as much as a month or more between exhibits, so be sure to call before visiting.

☐ Anacostia Park

1900 Anacostia Drive. (202) 433-1152. Open daily 6 A.M. to dusk. Closed Christmas Day.

This 750-acre park straddles both sides of the Anacostia River. In addition to the parkland, there's a swimming pool operated by the city's Recreation Department, basketball courts, and a roller-skating rink that is open from 1 P.M. to dusk, Monday through Friday. Free skates are available for children under 13. The park affords plenty of room for a picnic, and a mini playground lies adjacent to the picnic area.

☐ Congressional Cemetery

18th and E streets. (202) 543-0539. Open daily dawn to dusk. Free admission, but contributions are accepted (in the form of cash or your time and energy).

The oldest national cemetery in the United States is open for a visit, a picnic, dog walking, jogging, or a tour. You can even hold a wedding, baptism, or party in the recently restored stone chapel. John Hanley, of the Association for the Preservation of the Historic Congressional Cemetery, usually is at the cemetery from 6 A.M. to 10 P.M. to help you find your way around the place. Hanley will give a tour, or give you a brochure that lists who is buried where. He a notorious jokester. His favorite outing, it seems, is at Halloween time, when on a Saturday afternoon a haunted vault is opened up, ghost stories are told, and there are games, band music, and a barbecue. Come in costume, if you wish.

The cemetery contains the graves of congressional members, military officers, Indians, mass-accident victims, several criminals, and a variety of ordinary and not-so-ordinary citizens, including composer John Philip Sousa, Civil War photographer Mathew Brady, and J. Edgar Hoover.

Also buried here is Leonard Matlovich, who died in 1988. His grave is neatly covered with white gravel and flags wave briskly in the breeze above it. To refresh your memory, the following is etched on his gravestone: "They gave me a medal for killing two men, and a discharge for loving one."

☐ **Washington Navy Yard**

Ninth and M streets. (202) 433-2218. Navy Museum, Building 76, (202) 433-2651 (recording), (202) 433-4882. Marine Corps Museum, Building 58, (202) 433-3534. Navy and Marine Corps museums are open Monday through Friday 9 A.M. to 5 P.M., Saturday, Sunday, and federal holidays 10 A.M. to 5 P.M.; open late on Wednesday night in summer when the Navy Band is presenting The American Sailor concert. Guided tours are available. The U.S.S. Barry, (202) 433-3377, is open daily for self-guided tours 10 A.M. to 5 P.M. The U.S. Navy Combat Art Center, Building 67, Washington Navy Yard, (202) 433-3815, is open daily 8 A.M. to 4 P.M. Closed federal holidays. No guided tours.

Several options are available in this historic yard: the Navy Museum, the U.S.S. Barry Museum, the U.S. Navy Combat Art Center, and the Marine Corps Museum.

Of all the 4,000 navy-related historic objects—paintings, photographs, ship models, and weapons, ranging from cannons to a replica of the first atomic bomb—what seems to fascinate big and little children most at the yard are the three operating periscopes through which they can view the outside world. The second most popular activity appears to be sitting on antiaircraft guns and pretending to destroy the enemy, or at least to save us all from annihilation and destruction.

Another favorite stop at the yard is the U.S.S. Barry Museum, providing adventure and playground all in one. The Barry (DD 933) is a decommissioned navy destroyer now on permanent duty at the navy yard. Children can poke their noses into just about every corner of the ship, exploring the mess, galleys, officers quarters, engine rooms, and guns. They can even sit in the captain's chair. Imaginations soar at the homing torpedo attached to a rocket motor.

Artists have recorded the story of naval and marine units at sea and ashore, in war and in peace, since before World War II. Military action, launchings, explorations, and sailings have often been captured on canvas. Artworks on these subjects are exhibited at the U.S. Navy Combat Art Center, and each year the collection increases by approximately 150 canvases. Changing exhibits are on display all year.

An hour-long concert, The American Sailor, is presented in the amphitheater by the Navy Band at 9 P.M. every Wednesday throughout the summer. For free concert reservations call (202) 433-2218.

The Marine Corps Museum offers a chronological regimental history of the Marine Corps from 1775. Models, dioramas, and various weapons, including cannons from the 1800s, are on display. Older children probably will enjoy this museum more than younger children.

An annual Seafaring Celebration is scheduled in early November with music, storytelling, fortune-telling, and model making, scrimshaw, and hat making demonstrations.

☐ **Marine Barracks**

Eighth and I streets. (202) 433-6060. Park at Washington Navy Yard and take free shuttle bus service.

Every Friday night from May through August, there's an evening parade, or tattoo. Admission is free, but advance seating reservations are a must. Call for reservations between 8 and 11 A.M. and 1 and 3 P.M. Monday through Thursday, preferably three weeks ahead of desired date.

The gates are opened at 8:30 P.M. After all reservation holders have been admitted, those without reservations who are waiting outside the main gate are offered any remaining seats. An 8:45 P.M. concert opens the event and it is followed by the drills, a 75-minute performance of music and precision marching by the U.S. Marine and Bugle Corps and the Marine Corps Silent Drill Platoon. Bring a camera with fast film if you want to catch this stirring sight.

Northeast Washington

☐ Kenilworth Aquatic Gardens

1900 Anacostia Avenue at Douglas Street. (202) 426-6905 (recording). Gardens are open daily 7 A.M. to dusk; visitor center closes at 4 P.M. Guided tours are given daily from Memorial Day to Labor Day at 9 A.M., 11 A.M., and 1 P.M., 60 to 90 minutes long, depending upon your interests and the questions asked.

This is the only national park dedicated entirely to water-loving plants. If you arrive in the morning you can see the night-blooming water lilies before they close and the day lilies as they open. It seems as if every water lily and plant in existence is here, including the imposing South American Victoria amazonica. Its leaves, which are like platters with upturned edges, can extend to six feet in diameter, large enough to hold a 90-pound child. The wetlands are not only home to plants, but also to animals: turtles, snakes, fingernail-sized frogs, bullfrogs, insects, mosquito fish, muskrats, migratory birds, ducks, and red-winged blackbirds.

About mid-June you may see as many as 70 varieties of day-blooming water lilies; in late July and early August the day- and night-blooming tropical water lilies are at their peak. Special environmental education programs are offered. There is a small art gallery featuring the plants and blooms of the gardens. Bring your camera and plenty of film. Picnic tables provide a good place to stop for lunch.

The visitor center is wheelchair accessible and displays photographs and related artworks about the gardens.

☐ United States National Arboretum

3501 New York Avenue. (202) 475-4815. Open Monday through Friday 8 A.M. to 5 P.M., weekends 10 A.M. to 5 P.M. Closed Christmas Day. National Bonsai Collection is open daily 10 A.M. to 2:30 P.M.

Occupying 444 acres, the arboretum has nine miles of paved roadway that lead visitors to the various plant collections and gardens. Of particular note to little ones is the National Bonsai Collection, which features trees that are more to their size. Children also like to see the aquatic gardens (close to the parking lot), home to numerous lilies and some 400 Nishiki koi (the large, colorful carp). Pick up the little brochure that details all manner of trivia, such as the fact that the fish ate 2,600 pounds of food in 1989. The fish are fed from the back terrace at 12:30 P.M. from April to November. Do not bring food from home (it isn't good for them). Children will be given food to feed the fish.

Peak flowering season at the arboretum is in late April and May, when the azaleas (among the most extensive collection in the nation), flowering dogwoods, crabapples, mountain laurels, peonies, elephant-ear magnolias, and old roses present their fashion show. In the fall, tulip poplars and hickories present rich yellow leaves and gums and dogwoods turn red and bronze, creating a beautiful fall foliage display.

The herb garden is interesting because the plants on display demonstrate the significance of herbs in the everyday lives of ordinary people. In the specialty garden, for instance, you can see which plants are used for dyes, medicine, cooking, fuel, oil, pesticides, fibers, fragrances, and beverages.

The Capitol Columns, removed from the Capitol building in the 1950s as part of the east portico expansion, are another arboretum focal point. They date to the early 1800s, and each one weighs five tons and stands 34 feet tall. After 28 years of storage, they were moved to the arboretum grounds in the mid-1980s.

Views of the Anacostia River and other Washington sites are available at the Kingman Lake and Hickey Hill overlooks. Picnicking is permitted in the arboretum in designated areas.

□ United States Post Office

900 Brentwood Road. (202) 636-1208. One-hour walk-in tours are given Tuesday through Friday 9:30 A.M. to 7 P.M.; 24-hour notice is advised, particularly for groups.

Mail no more comes from a post office than milk comes from a grocery store, yet it is gathered, sorted, and sent upon its way here. More than 5 million pieces a day are sent off to mail boxes around the world just from this operation.

The tour, which can be noisy because of all the machinery, first takes you past the collected mail arriving at the loading docks. Here the mail is transferred from trucks to robot-driven bins. The machines separate packages and thick envelopes from thin envelopes, or "flats." Conveyer belts keep the mail flowing, up and down, in and out, turning, dropping, through funnels and slots, until it arrives at the cancellation machines. You can follow packages or mail or both at that fork.

Even with the knowledge of what computers and machinery should be able to do today, it's still amazing that machines can read the address of a letter, check its ZIP code and destination for concurrence, cancel the stamp, and send it on its way to the tune of 9 letters a second, 54 letters a minute, 3,240 letters an hour, 194,400 letters a day.

☐ National Shrine of the Immaculate Conception

Michigan Avenue and Fourth Street. (202) 526-8300. Open daily 7 A.M. to 7 P.M. April 1 through October 31, 7 A.M. to 6 P.M. November 1 through March 31. Guided tours (about 45 minutes long) are given every half hour from 9 to 11 A.M. and 1 to 3 P.M. Monday through Saturday, 1:30 to 4 P.M. Sunday. The gift shop is open daily, and the cafeteria is open daily for breakfast and lunch. Brookland/Catholic University subway station.

The shrine, the largest Roman Catholic church in the United States, has 57 chapels, 176 stained-glass windows, and many icons, statues, mosaics (one of the most extensive collections in the world), domes, and vaults. Its architecture represents the Byzantine and Romanesque styles of two thousand years ago.

☐ Franciscan Monastery

1400 Quincy Street. (202) 526-6800. Open daily 8 A.M. to 5 P.M. Free admission, but contributions are accepted. Guided tours (about 45 minutes long) are given Monday through Saturday on the hour 9 to 11 A.M. and 1 to 4 P.M., Sunday 1 to 4 P.M.

The tour explains the interior of the monastery's Memorial Church and includes the catacombs, which are a reproduction of the Roman catacombs where Christians hid and worshipped in secret to avoid persecution. Children particularly like the catacombs, giving their reasons as "spooky," "mysterious" and "neat."

The beautiful grounds come into full living color during the rose season, for the monastery reportedly has one of the largest rose gardens in the country. They even grow roses here that bloom in December. Along the garden walks are the Stations of the Cross and replicas of the shrines at Bethlehem and Lourdes. Easter service is said to be very moving and inspirational.

☐ Dance Place

3225 Eighth Street. (202) 269-1600. Brookland/Catholic University subway station.

Carla Perlo's dream come true. Carla and Dance Place are the foremost presenters of contemporary dance in Washington. Performances are given almost every weekend, with ticket prices set at $10 general admission, and $8 for senior citizens, students, and members. Classes are regularly scheduled for longterm visitors or residents interested in contemporary dance. Children's performances are scheduled on

Saturday afternoons. Admission for adults is $5 and children are admitted free.

☐ Capital Children's Museum

800 Third Street at H Street. (202) 543-8600. Open daily 10 A.M. to 5 P.M. Closed Easter, Thanksgiving, and Christmas New Year's days. Admission, $5; senior citizens over 59, $2; children under 2, free. Union Station subway station.

This museum, which is primarily aimed at elementary-school children, is a hands-on learning laboratory where children can touch and play with exhibits. There is an interactive exhibit about sound and deafness, and a Mexican village where visitors can make tortillas and paper flowers and necklaces. Children can also climb through mock sewers, work on computers, dial telephones, play in the grocery store, slide down a fire pole, be enclosed in a bubble, tape a television commercial, feed Rosie the goat, take flight with Superman, make a printer's newspaper hat, learn to juggle, and countless other things that kids enjoy doing.

People have complained for some time that the museum is not air-conditioned and can be nearly intolerable in Washington's summer heat and humidity. Part of the museum is air-conditioned, and they're working on the rest.

☐ Union Station

40 Massachusetts and Delaware avenues. (202) 289-1908. Train station operations are open daily 24 hours. Retail shops are open Monday through Saturday 10 A.M. to 9 P.M., Sunday 12 noon to 6 P.M. Some station eateries open to serve early Metrorail and Amtrak riders and visitors. Full-service restaurants stay open for late dining. Parking garage. Union Station subway station.

This is the largest waiting room of its kind in the world. Amtrak, MARC (Maryland Rail Commuters train system), light-rail commuter services from Fredericksburg and Manassas (starting late 1991, 703-524-3322), Metrorail, and Old Town Trolley all stop here, and a couple of automobile rental agencies have offices in the station.

It's difficult to believe that this grand station, which opened in 1907 and basically closed in 1981, was allowed to deteriorate so much that rain damage caused part of the roof to collapse and toadstools started growing inside. For a while there was a visitor center that almost no one visited. Now, the station features a large festival marketplace, with 25 eateries (fast-foot options from sushi to hotdogs and pizza to hamburgers), boutiques, and nine movie theaters (you can even charge your movie ticket). Look for the large clock in the Main Hall, just over the entrance to the East Hall. It uses "IIII" at the point where most Roman numeral clocks would use "IV." That's the way it was when the station opened, and that's the way the restorers kept it.

Activities are scheduled at the station throughout the year. During the holiday season a miniature train setup, measuring a huge 16 by 32 feet, is erected. Four half-inch scale trains lead the viewers' eyes through a quaint village with scale people, trees, trolley cars, and bridges; an industrial site; a small town; and a rural area with scale model farming equipment. The setup, which includes period automobiles, sits beneath snow-capped mountains in a scene reminiscent of Currier and Ives. The model trains are executed with standard LGB body styling finished in slate black and red, yellow, blue, and green.

For fine dining there's Michael's Adirondacks (a grand eating experience, particularly if you're dining on someone else's expense account), America (backlit maps of the states, with specialties from almost every state), Center Cafe (two-tiered restaurant with a continental menu emphasizing seafood), Pizzeria Uno (gourmet pizza, soups, salads, burgers, and sandwiches), Sfuzzi (pronounced fuzzi with a long u and offering not-so-run-of-the-mill Italian food amidst great decor), and Station Grill (old-time bar and grill in the classic tradition of Victorian hardwoods and tin ceiling).

A five-story, 1,400-car parking garage with long-term facilities rises behind the station. Parking is free for two hours to shop customers and for three hours for moviegoers. Prepare to show your movie stub or stamped ticket when you exit the garage.

☐ Lincoln Park

East Capitol Street, between 11th and 13th streets.

In the middle of this park is a bronze statue of Abraham Lincoln and a newly freed slave, just rising from his knees and grasping a broken chain. It celebrates the abolition of slavery in the District of Columbia, and the statue was paid for with contributions from hundreds of former slaves who wanted to pay tribute to the man who had proclaimed their freedom in 1863. The freedman was Archer Alexander, a Virginia-born slave, and his rescuer was the Rev. William Greenleaf Eliot, grandfather of poet and playwright T. S. Eliot.

Maryland

Choose from zoos, museums and galleries, professional sports, space programs, farms, ethnic festivals, boating, and the ocean. Maryland offers a little bit of everything. The following are some of the favorite things for children, listed alphabetically by city.

Baltimore

One interesting way to see Baltimore is via the **water taxis**, which make 11 stops: Maryland Science Center, Federal Hill, Inner Harbor Marina, Harborview, Museum of Industry, Fells Point, Harris Creek, Canton Waterfront Park, Pier Five (concert pavilion), National Aquarium, and Harborplace. Most of these stops are convenient to tourist spots around the city.

The schedule operates from 11 A.M. to 9 P.M. Sunday through Thursday and 11 A.M. to 12 midnight on Friday, Saturday, and holidays in April, September, and October; and 11 A.M. to 11 P.M. from May through August. Cost is $3.25 for adults and $2.25 for children under ten with an adult; the ticket is good the entire day of purchase. Service can be suspended during thunderstorms and lightning.

☐ Inner Harbor

Inner Harbor, the renovated and restored area around the harbor, has a number of fascinating places to visit. There's the Baltimore Maritime Museum, the Baltimore Public Works Museum and Streetscape, Federal Hill (great for a view of the harbor), Harborplace (a festival marketplace filled with eateries and shops), the Maryland Science Center and Davis Planetarium (see below), the National Aquarium in Baltimore (see below), the U.S. Frigate *Constellation* (see below), and Top of the World, for another view of the area (charge).

☐ National Aquarium

Pier 3, 501 East Pratt Street. (301) 576-3810. Open daily 10 A.M. to 5 P.M., Friday until 8 P.M. with reduced Friday night admissions (and fewer people); extended summer hours. Closed Christmas and New Year's days. Adults, $10.75; students, senior citizens, and active-duty military personnel, $8.50; children 3 to 11, $6.50. Guided tours are given for groups of 20 or more by prior arrangement. Membership available.

There are two absolute favorite places here children like to visit, the seal pool where harbor and gray seals play in an outdoor 70,000-gallon rock pool (you don't even have to pay to see it or to watch the regular daily feedings at 10 A.M., 1 P.M., and 4 P.M.) and the shark tank in the Open Ocean Exhibit inside. This is no small-sardine shark tank. It holds 220,000 gallons of water, as well as lemon, sand tiger, sandbar, and nurse sharks and large game fish. Visiting the shark tank and the 335,000-gallon Atlantic Coral Reef exhibit, which are behind 13-foot-high windows, is like snorkeling among the most beautiful and dangerous creatures of the deep. Three times a day, divers plunge in to hand-feed hundreds of fish, rays, and a Hawksbill turtle.

The Sea Cliffs exhibit re-creates the cliffs of Heimay, Iceland, and is the only display in the country that features three species of subarctic seabirds. Daily feedings and educational presentations of puffins, murres, and razorbills take place at 11 A.M. and 3:30 P.M. Of particular note is that the glass is one-way, so the birds don't see the people looking in and the people noises do not penetrate.

Little children like to stop by the Children's Cove, where the North American Tidal Pools allow them to touch and hold such little critters as horseshoe crabs, sea urchins, and starfish. The aquarium also has a South American rain-forest exhibit with exotic birds and lots and lots of humidity.

During the summer, volunteer guides walk around the aquarium holding things for visitors to touch and feel, such as the saw from a sawtooth shark, the jaw from a shark, and the disk from a whale spine (aquarium officials think it's from the whale skeleton hanging atop the large central tank, which weighed a mere 60 tons when alive).

A new $35-million Marine Mammal Pavilion opened in late 1990 that showcases the majesty of dolphins and whales. Reached via an enclosed skywalk from the original aquarium, it is the most sophisticated installation of its type in the country and combines family entertainment with educational and participatory exhibitry. The centerpiece of the new pavilion is a 1.2 million-gallon pool and the 1,300-seat Lyn P. Meyerhoff Amphitheater, home to three beluga whales and six Atlantic bottlenose dolphins. Surrounding the pool are the world's largest acrylic windows. Electronic Vidiwalls, the first of their kind in any zoo or aquarium, project close up views of the marine mammals' unique characteristics. A discovery room has hands-on artifacts from shark's teeth and jaws to whale vertebrae.

Numerous special programs are offered at the aquarium throughout the year.

☐ Maryland Science Center

601 Light Street. (301) 685-5225 (recording), 685-2370 (office), 837-IMAX

(IMAX information). Open Monday through Friday 10 A.M. to 5 P.M., Saturday 10 A.M. to 8 P.M., Sunday 12 noon to 6 P.M.; extended summer hours. Friday and Saturday evenings are special IMAX presentations. Adults, $7.50; children 4 to 17, senior citizens, and active-duty military personnel, $5.50; children 3 and under, free; IMAX admission included; Davis Planetarium show an additional $2.

Three floors of activity here offer wonderful hands-on experiences that present science as a part of Maryland life.

The IMAX theater (40 by 75 feet) shows films on space exploration (*The Dream is Alive*), boating through the Grand Canyon, surfing in Hawaii, or other adventures that transport you without ever leaving your seat. I prefer a seat close to the front and near the screen to feel like the surf may actually splash on me; you may prefer sitting higher.

The planetarium is not recommended for very young children, but their older siblings will enjoy exploring the night skies through its various programs. Unfortunately, there's a lot of light pollution in the Washington-Baltimore area, which obliterates much of the night sky. Fortunately, this is the place to find those hidden stars.

Children particularly like several exhibits. A new one on structures lets them work with various-sized building blocks to create their own architecture and construction projects. A kid's room is designed for children three to seven years of age, who may not understand the more advanced scientific exhibits. Among the treasures in here are workshop tools; a nature table with bones, feathers, and skins; a dissecting scope through which can be seen the different stages of a tadpole changing into a frog; an ant farm; a sound table with noise makers; X-rays on a lighted table; books; and a computer with programs about shapes, counting, and the alphabet.

A television studio is available for children to tape themselves doing the weather or sports and then see how they look. An all-time favorite is the Demonstration Stage where children are asked to participate in scientific experiments dealing with chemistry, electricity, and other facets of science. Other displays deal with the Chesapeake Bay, energy, and space. An exhibit featuring a Hubble Space Telescope explains what's wrong with the one that's currently out in orbit.

The gift shop has everything from kaleidoscopes to holograms and is nearly as interesting as the museum.

☐ U.S. Frigate Constellation

Pier 1, Pratt Street. (301) 539-1797. Open Monday through Saturday 10 A.M. to 6 P.M., Sunday and holidays 12 noon to 6 P.M. May through Labor Day; Monday through Saturday 10 A.M. to 4 P.M., Sunday 12 noon to 5 P.M. the rest of the year. Closed Good Friday and Christmas and New Year's days.

Adults, $2; senior citizens, $1.50; children 6 to 15, $1. Guided tours are given daily every other hour on the hour.

Nicknamed the Yankee Racehorse, this frigate is the nation's elder warship. Launched in 1797, it fought pirates in Tripoli, Libya, in 1802; saw action in the War of 1812; and is the oldest surviving fighting vessel of the Civil War. It now is a museum berthed in the Baltimore harbor. The captain's cabin is particularly interesting, as are the gun emplacements and the fireplaces (on board a ship? yes!).

☐ Fort McHenry National Monument and Historic Shrine

East Fort Avenue. (301) 962-4290. Open daily 8 A.M. to 5 P.M., summer 8 A.M. to 8 P.M. Admission to fort buildings for adults, $1; children 16 and under and senior citizens 62 and over, free. Admission to grounds, free.

The fort is known as the place during the War of 1812 where, on the night of September 13, 1912, the flag flew that inspired Francis Scott Key to write the *Star-Spangled Banner*. A 16-minute movie about the Battle of Baltimore and the writing of the national anthem is shown every 30 minutes on the hour and half hour. At its conclusion, the national anthem commences and the curtain on the right-hand wall opens to reveal a humongous flag, measuring 30 by 42 feet. Everyone stands, of course, which is great planning because that's when you're supposed to leave the building and go into the center of the fort.

The fort played an important part in history before and after the War of 1812. During the Civil War it was a prison camp and during World War I it was a large army hospital base. Exhibits explain the fort's uses over the years.

Children particularly love the cannons and the cannonballs. They're never fired, but during the summer people are dressed in replica uniforms from the War of 1812 and go through the drills and duties of garrisoning a fort in those days. Visitors can talk with them and ask questions, as well as see the barracks, the powder magazine, and the flagpole.

The fort grounds are nice for a picnic and a little exercise.

☐ Walters Art Gallery

600 North Charles Street at Mount Vernon Square. (301) 547-ARTS (recording), (301) 547-9000. Open Tuesday through Sunday 11 A.M. to 5 P.M. Closed Monday, the Fourth of July and Thanksgiving, Christmas Eve, Christmas and New Year's days. Adults, $2; senior citizens, $1; members, students with valid identification cards, and children under 18, free; free admission on Wednesday.

This extraordinary collection ranges over a 5,000-year period, from ancient Egypt to art nouveau, with a hefty helping of the decorative arts and illuminated manuscripts. Young warriors will be particularly entranced in the Arms and Armor Gallery with its ferocious weaponry and gleaming uniforms. Oh the battles to be fought with a trusty lance and a mighty crossbow!

On the first Saturday of the month there is a preschoolers' program, usually a short tour, story, and simple art projects, that explores a single theme such as the seasons or animals.

Monthly workshops are held for six to nine year olds and their parents. Participants may make books, discover architecture, see a variety of endangered animals as depicted by artists through the ages, or work with stained glass. Other workshops and activities are scheduled for older children and family members. Storyteller Rachmiel Tobesman spins tales in various galleries, and the Children's Theatre Association presents plays and sponsors appearances by Umoja Sasa, an African story troupe.

Some activities require advance reservations, and some have a charge or a requested donation.

☐ B & O Railroad Museum

901 West Pratt Street, at Poppleton Street. (301) 752-2490 (information), (301) 752-2461 (administrative office). Open Tuesday through Sunday 10 A.M. to 4 P.M., Thursday until 8 P.M. in June, July, and August. Adults, $5; students age 5 through college, $3; senior citizens 60 and over, $4; children 4 and under, free.

As you walk from your car to the museum entrance, note the tracks that were the first long-distance railroad tracks laid in America, in 1830. This was the location of the Mount Clare Station, the oldest railroad station in the country and the birthplace of the B & O Railroad. On the grounds and in the 1884 roundhouse are 110 full-sized trains, an extensive and fascinating H.O. scale-model train, an extraordinary collection of model bridges, ancient fire-engine cars, and the tools that were used to lay the rail network for a modern nation. Among the museum's treasured exhibits is a replica of the famous Tom Thumb steam-powered vehicle built by Peter Cooper in 1829. This vast collection of freight cars, cabooses, locomotives, primitive cars, Conestoga wagons, and other vehicles on wheels always delights children of all ages.

The museum is the largest institution of railroad equipment in the United States.

☐ Babe Ruth Birthplace

Baltimore Orioles Museum, 216 Emory Street. (301) 727-1539. Open daily 10 A.M. to 5 P.M. April through October, 10 A.M. to 4 P.M. November through

March. Closed Easter, Christmas, Thanksgiving, and New Year's days. Adults, $3; senior citizens, $2; children 5 through 12, $1.50; children 4 and under, free.

America's second largest baseball museum (after the Baseball Hall of Fame Museum) is filled with memorabilia of the Babe, the Orioles, and Maryland baseball, although the Orioles part of the museum will move to separate quarters when the new stadium opens in 1992, just a short distance away. A 25-minute film documents Babe's early years and covers his time in baseball from 1914 to April 1948.

Baseball fanatics can get their fill of balls, bats, old uniforms, and trophies. Radios play tapes of the Sultan of Swat hitting the first home run in the newly opened Yankee Stadium in 1923 and his record-breaking 60th home run in 1927. An old-time outfield fence has 714 plaques, one for each of Ruth's home runs—listing the place and date of the run and the pitcher who pitched it—mounted on it.

Children's parties can be held here. If you schedule the party during the baseball season, reserve the space at least two months in advance, and make a contribution to the museum, the Orioles Bird will visit and sign autographs. Call (301) 243-9800 to make arrangements.

☐ Baltimore Museum of Art

Art Museum Drive. (301) 396-7101, (301) 396-6320 (Education Office). Open Tuesday, Wednesday, and Friday 10 A.M. to 4 P.M.; Thursday 10 A.M. to 7 P.M.; weekends 11 A.M. to 6 P.M. Adults, $3; children 18 and under, free; free admission on Thursday. Children's tours are given Tuesday through Friday 10 A.M. to 2 P.M.

One of the the highlights here is the collection of 18th- and 19th-century American artists. Children in particular like the historic Cheney Miniatures Rooms (living rooms, silver room, English parlor); the modern collection, because of the generally large scale of the works and their vibrant colors; a Martin Pureyor wooden sculpture that takes up the entire Fox Court; the African collection that's installed close to the ground, at child level; a pre-Columbian collection of little dolls; and the Wurtzburger Sculpture Garden with pieces by Calder, Moore, and Rodin.

☐ Baltimore Zoo

Druid Hill Park, off exit 7 of Interstate 83. (301) 366-5466 (recording), 396-7102 (administration). Open daily 10 A.M. to 4:20 P.M.; extended summer hours. Closed Christmas Day. Adults $5; children 2 to 11 and senior citizens, $3; children under 2, free; free admission for all children Saturday until 12 noon.

Of particular interest is the Lyn T. Meyerhoff Maryland Wilderness and Discovery Path, reached through the Children's Zoo, that captures the various Maryland biomes. You can sit in an oriole's nest, step on giant lily pads, walk under a frolicking otter, poke your head up a woodchuck hole, work your way across a swinging bridge, climb a tree as you explore its habitat and slide down from the top of an enormous fallen limb, and visit barnyard animals.

The zoo also boasts the most productive colony of African blackfooted penguins in the United States; a naturalistic habitat for African elephants; some rare and unusual animals, such as the red panda (arguably part of the panda family, but generally accepted as part of the species), the sitatunga antelope, lion-tailed macaques, and golden-lion tamarins; and my favorite bird because of its pretty head feathers, the African crown crane. A new African Watering Hole, a refuge for the endangered white rhinoceros, and habitats for zebras, antelopes, and ostriches are under construction as of this writing.

Times for the penguin feeding and the African elephant demonstrations are posted. Pony rides are available during the summer at the Children's Zoo, as is the carousel and the Zoo-Choo train.

The zoo, established in 1876, is the third oldest in the nation and many of the cages reflect the thinking of zoo procedures of those days, updated a little.

A tram is available for 25 cents per person to take weary walkers from one part of the zoo to another. Have your hand stamped and ride the tram all day.

Brooklandville

☐ Cloisters Children's Museum

10440 Falls Road. (301) 823-2550, (301) 823-2551 (schedules and tickets to special events). Open Wednesday through Friday 10 A.M. to 4 P.M., Saturday and Sunday 12 noon to 4 P.M. Adults and children, $3; senior citizens, $2.

This Tudor mansion with Gothic Revival touches is designed and sized for children to learn and play through art activities, workshops, performances, and hands-on fun rather than high-tech science displays. Imagination rules here, starting with the griffins that guard the entrance and the human and animal gargoyles that oversee the walls. Children can don costumes, play musical instruments, create lives in antique dollhouses, build structures with wooden blocks, or just crawl into a comfortable reading nook under the third-floor eaves for a literary journey into their favorite book. They can climb into a book and slide out, mail a letter from a post office, live in a make-believe village, conduct a wooden train, and pilot a barge against a Baltimore harbor backdrop.

Outdoors, the wooded property is home to a butterfly garden and a menagerie of animals, including deer, owls, porcupines, quail, rabbits, and wild turkeys. Three marked nature trails vary in length from a quarter mile to one mile.

Scheduled activities range from nature walks, visual scavenger hunts, and concerts to an antique car show.

Ellicott City

☐ B & O Railroad Station Museum

Maryland Avenue and Main Street. (301) 461-1944 (recording). Open Friday through Monday 11 A.M. to 5 P.M.; last admission at 4 P.M. Closed on school holidays and during weather emergencies (snow). Adults, $4; children 5 to 12, $3; senior citizens, $2; children under 5, free.

This was the first passenger terminus of the B & O Railroad. There is a sight-and-sound show with a working model rail display, a restored 1927 caboose, and a visitor center. Ellicott City (Route 144) is an old mill town and many original stone buildings and fine examples of early mill workers' homes are still here. Antique and specialty shops are abundant.

Frederick

☐ Rose Hill Manor: Children's Museum and Park

1161 North Market Street. (301) 694-1648, (301) 694-1646. Open Monday through Saturday 10 A.M. to 4 P.M., Sunday 1 to 4 P.M. April through mid-December. Adults, $3; senior citizens and children under 17, $1.

Colonial crafts are demonstrated throughout the year, and children are encouraged to touch the various exhibits in the many buildings, including the blacksmith shop, carriage museum, farm museum, ice house, log cabin, and manor house. The aim of the museum is to make the 19th century come alive for children. And the best place to do this is in the room with the arts and crafts, toys, and costumes to try on. There should be museums and parks like this for adults.

Gaithersburg

☐ **National Institute of Standards and Technology** (formerly the Bureau of Standards)

Quince Orchard and Clopper Road. (301) 975-3585. Guided tours are given Thursday at 9:30 A.M. by appointment only.

The world's largest measurement laboratory is housed in a 21-building complex on 570 acres of land. It provides the basic standards for measuring length, time, mass, and temperature. The laboratory's research and development practices are in the fields of chemistry, engineering, and physics, and it assists in the solving of technological problems. Given that, you'll understand that the tours are very technical and liable to bore easily those who are not scientifically oriented.

The museum is a little more approachable for non-Einstein types and includes displays of scientific apparatus, important memorabilia, exhibits about current research, and historic documents concerning the science of measurement.

Glen Echo

☐ **Glen Echo Park**

7300 MacArthur Boulevard. (301) 492-6282 (recording); (301) 492-6663 (carousel). Open daily from 6 A.M. to 1 A.M. Closed Christmas and New Year's days.

What do you want from a park? A half-century-old carousel? A puppet theater? A children's theater? An art gallery of local artists? A Spanish Ballroom with dancing four or more nights a week from spring through late fall? Picnicking? This is the place.

Glen Echo Park used to be an amusement park and anyone who has been around here for more than a few years can tell you about the roller coaster, bumper cars, the fun house, and the miracles that occurred here, like falling in love under a full moon.

Greater miracles have happened. Following years of neglect, the park now belongs to the National Park Service. People have been working hard to restore it so our children can have wonderful memories here, too.

The carousel, a Dentzel, has been at the park since 1921, and is one of 27 remaining Dentzels in the United States and Canada. It has two chariots and 52 hand-carved figures (of which 36 are "jumpers"), including 40 horses, four ostriches, four rabbits, a deer, a tiger, a lion, and a giraffe. It usually operates April through October from Monday through Thursday 10 A.M. to 5 P.M., Friday through Sunday 12 noon to 6 P.M. If the carousel is the only reason you're going to the park, call ahead to confirm that it's running. It costs 50 cents. Children under eight must be accompanied by an adult. Park rangers have even been known to give a 20-minute carousel tour that explains the history of the ride.

Adventure Theater presents fairy tales and other children's stories every Saturday and Sunday at 1:30 and 3:30 P.M. Admission is $4.50 and reservations are suggested. The Puppet Company performs several times a day, several times a week. Tickets are $4. The Glen Echo Dance Theater is the resident dance company at the park, with regularly scheduled classes and performances.

Greenbelt

☐ **National Aeronautics and Space Administration(NASA)/ Goddard Space Flight Center**

Visitor Center and Museum, Soil Conservation Road. (301) 286-8981.
Visitor center is open Wednesday through Sunday, 10 A.M. to 4 P.M. Guided tours are given Wednesday, Thursday, and Friday at 2:30 P.M.

Goddard is the hub of NASA tracking activities, the center of the nation's space exploration program. It welcomes visitors to relive old space shots via films, exhibits, and interactive computers. The guided tour, which runs 30 to 40 minutes, takes visitors through the testing facility, the spacecraft control center, and other areas. No matter how many space launches you've watched on television, you're sure to be overwhelmed by the seemingly measureless array of computers, monitors, and state-of-tomorrow technology at this center.

Outside, in the rocket garden, you can see a Delta launch vehicle, a scale model of a lunar vehicle, and other representatives of outer-space voyages. A model rocket launch is held at 1 P.M. on the second Sunday of every month.

Community Day, held in mid-September, admits visitors to areas normally closed to the general public. This special tour stops at both the Nascom Division Center and the Spacecraft Systems Development and Integration Facility. The latter is one of the largest "clean rooms" in the world, with 86,000 square feet of contamination-free environment for building large payloads. Of particular importance and interest are the various everyday applications that space-shots research has produced. Model rocket launches, international ham-radio demonstrations, and musical entertainments also are on the program.

Kensington

☐ Washington Mormon Temple Visitors Center

9900 Stoneybrook Drive. (301) 587-0144. Open daily 10 A.M. to 9:30 P.M.

Called "one of the world's most technologically advanced religious exhibits," the temple is closed to non-Mormons, but much of the temple's beauty and spirit are to be found in the visitors center. For several weeks starting in late November, there are hundreds of thousands of tiny colored lights decorating the trees and bushes around the temple. This is a favorite photographic spot starting shortly before sundown. Carolers perform songs of the season, and concerts begin at 7:30 P.M.

Ocean City

Maryland's only seaside resort community has a ten-mile stretch of wide, sandy beaches and plenty of fishing (it's known as the White Marlin Capital of the World) and watersports (sailing, jet skiing, water skiing, parasailing, and windsurfing, particularly in the bay waters). On weekends, the little more than three-hour drive from Washington and Baltimore to Ocean City can become almost hopelessly jammed with traffic, so a midweek visit is best. Also, the weather stays milder longer than in the city, so a visit before Memorial Day and after Labor Day will still find some activity. Numerous festivals are scheduled throughout the year, and there are several amusement parks with rides and water slides.

Oxon Hill

☐ Oxon Hill Children's Farm

6411 Oxon Hill Road. (301) 839-1177 (recording). Open daily 8:30 A.M. to 5 P.M.

This is a turn-of-the century farm with chickens, cows, pigs, horses, vegetables, and demonstrations of farming practices and seasonal arts and crafts of the early 1900s. You can watch wheat threshing, corn picking, molasses cooking, sorghum-syrup making, and sheep shearing.

Cow milking is done every day at 10:30 A.M. and at 4 P.M., and egg gathering occurs at 2 P.M. Occasional farm chores and activities go on throughout the day. Obviously, some things are seasonal, such as the sheep shearing, so call if there's something in particular you want to see and you plan on being in the area for a while.

Guides and farm workers in period costumes are available as escorts, but visitors may walk around on their own and pet the animals, watch the farmers at work, or even help with the harvesting.

Potomac

☐ Great Falls Park

Off MacArthur Boulevard. Admission for each vehicle is $3; visitors who enter by motorcycle, bicycle, or on foot, $1; both admissions are good for seven days. Frequent park users can buy a $10 annual pass that provides unlimited year-long access to the park.

This long, linear park features mule-drawn barge rides along the historic C & O Canal, kayaking, hiking, and biking.

☐ C & O Canal Barge Rides

11710 MacArthur Boulevard. (301) 299-2026. Rides are available at Georgetown in Washington and here at Great Falls, from about mid-April through mid-October. Hours and days vary; summer barge trips depart Wednesday through Sunday at 10:30 A.M., 1 P.M., and 3 P.M.; reduced schedule in effect in spring and fall. Adults, $4; senior citizens (62 and over), $3; children 12 and under, $2.50.

Organized by the C & O Canal National Historical Park, the *Canal Clipper* carries you along a craggy river gorge and through the woods on a ride that recalls canal travel of a century ago. Guides wear period costumes and warn you against asking questions about things that happened after 1876, because theoretically this ride takes place then. The 90-foot boat is worked up and down lock 20 during the 90-minute ride; the process visually explains how boats are lifted and lowered from one water level to another. The living history works a little better here than on the barge trips in Georgetown, primarily because it is so quiet.

One-hour day trips and two-hour evening trips can be booked by groups, at special rates. Bring along a banjo or guitar and have an old-fashioned sing-along.

Prince Frederick

☐ **Battle Creek Cypress Swamp Sanctuary**

Grays Road off Route 506. (301) 535-5327. Open Tuesday through Saturday 10 A.M. to 5 P.M., Sunday 1 P.M. to 5 P.M. April through September, until 4:30 P.M. October through March. Closed Thanksgiving, Christmas, and New Year's days.

This is the largest northernmost stand of bald cypress. There's no Spanish moss hanging from the branches, and no southern belles in hoop skirts, but there is a wooden walkway through the swamp. Spring flowers are beautiful and the nature center has plenty of displays, including an occupied beehive. Special programs are held throughout most of the year.

Sharpsburg

☐ **Antietam National Battlefield**

Maryland Route 65, 5831 Dunker Church Road. (301) 432-5124. Open 8:30 A.M. to 5 P.M. in winter, 8 A.M. to 6 P.M. in the summer. Tours of the battlefield are given in summer if there is sufficient staffing.

Start your tour in the visitor center with the 26-minute film that is shown every hour on the hour. This is not a rehash of the battle, but is complementary to the driving tour. The political issues of the day are covered and the film includes Lincoln's visit here after the battle. A small museum shows a uniform, medical tools, and things that a private would have carried on him. An observation room displays three paintings done by Captain James Hope during the battle; a fourth painting is in the lobby. You can see about two thirds of the battlefield from the visitor center.

Antietam, which resulted in the largest number of deaths in any single day of any battle in which American soldiers have ever fought, marked Robert E. Lee's unsuccessful attempt to invade the North. The site offers plenty of gun embankments and fields of battle on which the imagination can re-create the Civil War. A driving tour is laid out just as the battle was fought, from morning through the cornfields, into the afternoon at Bloody Lane, and later at Burnside Bridge. A cassette describing the battle can be rented at the visitor center for $4, or purchased for $7.

Children who have studied this period of history will derive the most benefit from a visit and probably find it the most interesting.

Silver Spring

☐ Schaeffer's Piano Company

710 Sligo Avenue, and 8603 16th Street. (301) 589-3039. Open Monday through Friday 10 A.M. to 8 P.M., Saturday 10 A.M. to 6 P.M.

This piano company has been building fine instruments for about 90 years. At the Sligo Avenue building you'll find a warehouse and refurbishing area where you can see what goes into restoring a piano, including storage (grand piano lids are stored separately), working with keys and strings, stripping, brass polishing, tuning, and anything else that may be involved.

The 16th Street store is a salesroom, but there's a nickelodeon that they'll turn on for you so you can watch the drums drum and the keys key and the cymbals clang.

Suitland

☐ Paul E. Garber Facility

1000 Old Silver Hill Road. (202) 357-1400. Open for free three-hour guided tours Monday through Friday at 10 A.M. and 1 P.M. and weekends at 10 A.M. Reservations should be made two weeks in advance by calling the above number or by writing Tour Scheduler, National Air and Space Museum, Smithsonian Institution, Washington, D.C. 20960.

An open house usually is held during the last weekend in April, with aerospace-related demonstrations and activities, free concerts, and intergalactic views through telescopes. Garber joined the Smithsonian Institution in 1920 and is responsible for a great number of acquisitions, including Lindbergh's *Spirit of St. Louis.*

This suburban facility of the Smithsonian's Air and Space Museum is where restoration and preservation of classic and historic planes take place. Approximately 160 aircraft and numerous spacecraft, engines, propellers, and other flight-related objects are on display.

Included on the tour is a behind-the-scenes look at the restoration workshop, as well as two buildings of finished planes and two buildings of planes in pieces.

On weekdays and at the annual open house, visitors see craftsmen at work, sometimes refabricating missing pieces or hand-sanding a plane layer by layer. World War II aircraft, such as the *Enola Gay*, are the big draw. Other highlights are a MiG-15, Curtiss Jn-4D Jenny, Hawker Hurricane IIC, Vostok Spacecraft (a one-third scale model of the craft that carried Yuri Gagarin, the first man into space, on April 12, 1961), and a J-2 engine (one of the power packs for the Saturn launch vehicles).

The buildings are not heated or air-conditioned and you should wear comfortable shoes. There are no bathroom facilities available during the tour (there are for the open house). Young children certainly find the tour interesting, but because of its length it may be better to bring them to the open house, if you have that option.

Thurmont

☐ Catoctin Mountain Zoological Park

off U.S. 15. (301) 271-7488, (301) 662-2579. Open Monday through Thursday 9 A.M. to 6 P.M., Friday through Sunday 9 A.M. to 7 P.M. May through August, daily 9 A.M. to 5 P.M. September though April. Adults, $5.75; children 2 to 12, $4.25.

Over 400 native rare and endangered mammals, birds, and reptiles live here and participate in daily shows. Phase one of the North American Exhibit, which was opened in 1990, is a hands-on operation where visitors can touch the animals. If there is an education person or a volunteer in the teaching building, then the animals are outside the exhibit. If not, they're inside, and that happens primarily in the off-season. Children also can be involved in making arts and crafts.

Upper Marlboro

☐ Watkins Regional Park

301 Watkins Park Drive. (301) 249-6900, (301) 249-6202 (nature center). Open daily 7 A.M. to dusk. Closed Thanksgiving, Christmas, and New Year's days.

Plenty of facilities are available in the park, including a nature center, miniature-train ride, picnic grounds, campground, playground, an old-fashioned farm, an antique carousel, and in December, the annual Festival of Lights (no charge, but donations of food or money are accepted).

The nature center has regularly scheduled activities for all age groups, from studying animals and insects to hiking and basket making. Another strong draw is the pride and joy of the park, the hand-carved, hand-painted, 80-year-old carousel, which, along with the train ride, operates only in fair weather.

During the summer there's a $5 per car camping charge for people who do not live in Prince George's County or Montgomery County, Maryland.

Wheaton

☐ Wheaton Regional Park

2000 Shorefield Road. (301) 622-0056. Open daily dawn to dusk. Closed Thanksgiving, Christmas, and New Year's days.

In and around this area you will find a playground, picnic area, ballfields, carousel, farm, miniature train, nature center, and garden center.

The Herschell-Spillman carousel was manufactured between 1909 and 1915 and supposedly was designed to travel, because it could be assembled and disassembled in one day. It has 33 horses, three zebras, two chariots, and all the animals are "jumpers." The carousel is open during the warm season only; rides are 60 cents and parents who stand alongside seated children are admitted free.

Old MacDonald's Farm has chicks, ducklings, colts, piglets, a barn, a silo, a smokehouse, a bread oven, and a windmill. City folks who stop here can appreciate how a farm works.

On the playground there's a navy jet fighter to climb atop and slide down the other side, the Wheaton Stage Coach, pony rides, and a two-mile trip on a replica of a colorful 1865 steam-engine train.

☐ Brookside Nature Center

1400 Glenallen Avenue. (301) 946-9071. Open Tuesday through Saturday 9 A.M. to 5 P.M., Sunday 1 to 5 P.M. Guided tours by appointment only.

This center focuses on the natural history of metropolitan Washington, with attractions that include aquariums, an indoor turtle pool, an occupied beehive, slide shows, and movies.

□ Brookside Gardens

1500 Glenallan Avenue. (301) 949-8230 (recording). Grounds are open 9 A.M. to dusk; the two conservatories are open daily 9 A.M. to 5 P.M. Closed Christmas Day.

Within this 25-acre parkland are two conservatories filled with plants and flowers, including some exotic and foreign specimens. Outside are a number of public display gardens, including the following types: raised, azalea, formal (perennial, yew, rose), fragrance, trial, Japanese-style with teahouse, winter, aquatic, and butterfly.

At times you may see a blooming coffee tree, bananas, and chrysanthemums, or the annual Christmas flower show with such traditional seasonal plants as the Jerusalem cherry, cyclamen, and kalanchoe. Easter lilies, azaleas, hydrangeas, fuchsias, and dogwood are the stars of the spring flower show.

□ National Capital Trolley Museum

Bonifant Road between Layhill Road and New Hampshire Avenue. (301) 384-6088 (recording). Open Saturday, Sunday, Memorial Day, Fourth of July, and Labor Day 12 noon to 5 P.M.; until 9 P.M. Saturday and Sunday in December for Holly Trolley Illumination; Wednesday during July and August 12 noon to 4 P.M. Closed Christmas and New Year's days. Free admission; trolley rides are $1.50 for adults, $1 for children 2 through 18, free for children under 2. This is a complicated schedule to understand; call to make sure museum is open.

From Lincoln to Kennedy, Washington had streetcar trolleys. They disappeared in 1962.

For those who've never seen a trolley, or for those who miss them, this is a collection of American and European trolleys. It includes an 1889 Sweeper 07 that was used until 1962 to help maintain the Washington-area trolley system during snowy weather. An American deck-roof trolley of 1918 and vehicles from Vienna and Graz built in the early 1900s are in the collection. There's also a four-wheeled car of the Gay Nineties and a shiny streamliner.

A visitor center built to resemble an old-time railroad station is the boarding point for the trolley rides. Film programs are offered and you can purchase trolley-related items in the gift shop.

Virginia

According to the slogan coined by Virginia's tourism promoters, Virginia is for lovers. By that they mean lovers of the outdoors, history, arts, science, sports, or whatever it is that you love to do. You'll find plenty of things to love in this area. This section is organized alphabetically by city.

Alexandria

☐ **Torpedo Factory**

105 North Union Street. (703) 838-4565, (703) 683-0693 (tours). Open daily 10 A.M. to 5 P.M. Guided tours by appointment only.

The Torpedo Factory (that's what it used to be) is home to 150 artists dealing in prints, pottery, sculpture, glass, paint, and musical-instruments production. Children love the place because they can see work in progress and talk with the artists. No question is asked too often or left unanswered.

Three free sheets explain self-guided tours directed toward children, one for children 8 to 11, one for those 11 to 14, and a third for 14 to 18 year olds. An outside tour brochure (small charge) is designed for children 6 to 12.

The indoor tour for the youngest children is based on a mystery theme. Children are challenged with questions about shapes, colors, smells, and senses. The tour for the next oldest group, which involves journalistic techniques, encourages children to write an article about their observations and interviews. The high-school-level tour treats art as an avocation or an occupation. It suggests that teens select a medium and visit five artists to learn what they can about the art business.

Free hour-long, docent-led tours that relate the history of the building and focus on some of the artists can be arranged in advance and are suitable for children.

Arlington

☐ Arlington National Cemetery

Off Memorial Drive. (703) 692-0931, (703) 557-0613 (Arlington House). Open daily 9:30 A.M. to 4:30 P.M. October to March, until 6 P.M. April through September. Closed Christmas and New Year's days. Guided tours October through March by appointment only. Parking lot is $1 per hour for the first three hours, $2 per hour or portion thereof after that. Tourmobile stop. Arlington Cemetery subway station.

You are allowed to drive through the cemetery if you are attending a funeral or visiting a specific gravesite. In either case you have to obtain a special driving pass in the visitor center. To visit the cemetery otherwise, enter through the visitor center and pay $2.75 for adults and $1.25 for children to take the narrated 40-minute Tourmobile ride through the cemetery (of which at least 15 minutes is spent with boarding and unboarding at three stops along the route). Alternatively, you can walk. It's an uphill trek, but plenty of people do it. The Tourmobile stops are at the Kennedy gravesites, the Changing of the Guard, and at Arlington House (see following entry).

At the Kennedy gravesites you see the graves of John F. Kennedy, two of his children, and Robert F. Kennedy.

Also buried at Arlington are President and Chief Justice William Howard Taft, Supreme Court justices Earl Warren, Oliver Wendell Holmes, and William O. Douglas; Grand Canyon explorer John Wesley Powell, astronauts Dick Scobee and Michael Smith, sports figures Joe Louis and Abner Doubleday, and actor Lee Marvin.

At the Tomb of the Unknowns (with servicemen from World Wars I and II and the Korean and Vietnam conflicts), soldiers from the Third U.S. Infantry ("The Old Guard") stand guard 24 hours a day. The Changing of the Guard takes place every hour, on the hour, 8 A.M. to 5 P.M. from October 1 to March 31, and every half hour 8 A.M. to 7 P.M. from April 1 to September 30. At night the guard is changed every two hours. The guards take 21 steps before turning and facing the tomb for 21 seconds, corresponding to the 21-gun salute. The guards have taps, or "cheaters," on their shoe bottoms and on the insides of their shoe heels that make the snap of their salute sound so sharp.

Each year three major events are held in the 5,500-seat Memorial Amphitheater behind the Unknowns, Easter Sunrise Service, Memorial Day, and Veterans Day. Additionally, numerous veteran and civic groups hold memorial services throughout the year.

Nearby is the mast of the U.S.S. *Maine* and memorials honoring the crew from the space shuttle *Challenger* and the eight men who died in the 1980 Iran hostage rescue attempt.

□ Arlington House

On the grounds of Arlington National Cemetery. (703) 557-0613. Open daily 9:30 A.M. to 6 P.M. April through September, 9:30 A.M. to 4:30 P.M. October through March. Closed Christmas and New Year's days. Self-guided tours all year; candlelight tours in fall; special tours for the visually or hearing impaired by appointment only. Special observances are held on January 19, Lee's birthday, and on June 30, his wedding anniversary. Tourmobile stop.

This home was the residence of Robert E. Lee for more than 30 years. It fell into northern hands during the Civil War, and now is a tribute to the southern life style that just preceded the war. Many of the items—furniture, artwork, housewares—belonged to the Lee, Washington, and Custis families, or are excellent reproductions. From the portico (on the north side) there is a great view of Washington.

Upstairs are five bedrooms and a playroom. Lee's three youngest daughters shared a room and his three sons shared a second room; his oldest daughter had her own room. The playroom is filled with diminutive furniture, dolls, and toys of the 1800s.

Around Christmas, the house is decorated as it would have been while Lee lived there. Special events are held to celebrate the season.

□ Netherlands Carillon

Meade Street and Marshall Drive. (703) 285-2598.

Above the Arlington National Cemetery is this marvelous carillon, donated by the Dutch in gratitude for help from the United States during World War II. Its 127-foot-tall square tower contains 49 bells, and stands as a symbol of friendship between the two countries. The largest, or "bourdon," bell weighs 12,654 pounds and measures over six feet in diameter. The smallest is nine inches in diameter and weighs just 37-1/2 pounds. The large bells represent the adults of the Netherlands; the small ones symbolize the country's youth.

Concerts by such well-known carillonneurs as Frank Della Penna are presented on weekends and holidays. Call for the schedule.

□ United States Marine Corps War Memorial (Iwo Jima)

Adjacent to Arlington National Cemetery. (202) 433-6060.

The Marine Sunset Parade is held on Tuesday nights at 7 P.M. from June through August. This is a 75-minute performance of music and marching by the Marine Drum and Bugle Corps and the Marine Corps Silent Drill Platoon. Parking is available at the Arlington National

Cemetery ($1 per hour for the first three hours) and a free shuttle service to the parade grounds is provided by the marines, starting at 6 P.M. No reservations are necessary.

Many television crews will set up by this statue to cover Washington's annual Fourth of July fireworks celebration that takes place along the Mall. Bring a blanket, picnic, and plenty of friends.

Great Falls

☐ Great Falls National Park

9200 Old Dominion Drive. (703) 285-2966. Open daily 7 A.M. to dusk. Entrance fee per vehicle, $3.

Within the 800 square acres of this park you'll have the opportunity to enjoy nature and learn some of the history of the area. Tours are given at least once a day of the Patowmack Canal, the only civil-engineering project every worked on by George Washington. Along the way you'll stop by the old ghost town of Matildaville, and you'll enjoy a spectacular view of the Potomac River where it takes an exuberant 77-foot drop at Great Falls into Stephen Mather Gorge. Most East Coast falls do not drop all at one time, as Niagara Falls does. Instead they drop, as does Great Falls, in a series of rapids. At times, it's said, more water tumbles over this drop than over Niagara. The Great Falls section of the river can be very hazardous, so heed the signs and the rangers if you're contemplating swimming or boating.

☐ Riverbend Park and Nature Center

8814 Jeffrey Road. (703) 759-3211. Park is open daily dawn to dusk. Entrance fee per car, $4 during the busy season or on a particularly busy day; otherwise, free admission; free admission for Fairfax County residents. Nature center is open Wednesday through Monday 12 noon to 5 P.M. Closed Tuesday and on weekdays in January and February.

Part of the park, which is located next to Great Falls National Park, is a nature center with plenty of organized and unorganized activities, particularly for little youngsters. One of the favorites is the hike along a quarter-mile stroller-friendly route with eight stops to look for natural treasures. Reserve a discovery bag with a squirrel puppet, sniff boxes (sassafras and other aromatic things), and pictures to take along this Duff (stuff that accumulates on the forest floor) 'n' Stuff (and the stuff that goes with it) trail. Inside the center is a museum with changing exhibits that might include live snakes, fish, silkworm cocoons and eggs, birds and bird seed, or whatever else is seasonal.

The Paw Paw Passage is a winding, 1 1/4-mile-long trail that covers bridges, hills, and dales. Older children can search for tree fungi, mushrooms, and even a deer's jawbone along this path. While walking along the Potomac, you can watch kayakers shoot the rapids at Great Falls.

☐ **Roosevelt Island**

George Washington Memorial Parkway (accessible only from northbound lane, coming from Washington). (703) 285-2598. Open daily 7 A.M. to dusk. Guided tours for children and school groups by appointment only.

Accessible only by footbridge (there's a parking lot), the island is the site of a memorial to Theodore Roosevelt. An uphill, unpaved trail leads to the memorial, which includes a bronze statue of the former president and large granite stones with some of his thoughts etched on them. There is a moat and plenty of sitting space. Trails (swamp trail and highland trail) lead all the way around the island, which is home to a variety of birds, animals, and plants. Although approached from Virginia, the island is in Washington, and adults hoping to take advantage of the fishing opportunities will need to purchase a Washington fishing license; children under 16 do not need a license.

During the summer, one-day children's camps for 7 to 11 year olds are held on Wednesday from 8:30 A.M. to 3 P.M. You need to reserve a space and to provide an extra pair of really old and grungy sneakers, because the thing the kids love to do the most is participate in the swamp tromp, where they actually get into the swamp. They have some four to eight different activities from which to choose, including arts and crafts and a talk from the park police.

Herndon

☐ **The Washington and Old Dominion Railroad Regional Park**

5400 Ox Road, Fairfax Station (park office address). (703) 352-5900, (703) 437-1910 (trail office). Open 7 A.M. to dusk.

This is the skinniest and one of the longest parks in Virginia, measuring 45 miles long by 100 feet wide. The park stretches through three counties—Fairfax, Arlington, and Loudoun—from Shirlington to Leesburg along the former roadbed of the W & O D Railroad. You can walk it, run it, bike it, or track it on horseback. Along the way you'll find Parcours fitness stations and trails that lead off in all directions. There are numerous entrances to the park and the easiest way to decide what to do and where to do it is by calling the trail office and requesting a map. The cost is $4.50 by mail, $3.50 if you pick it up yourself.

Six old railroad stations and an old post office that is now a museum are located in the park. Located at mile marker 20, the museum has a statue out front of William Lewis Herndon, a U.S. Navy captain whose name became attached to the post office in 1859. Inside the museum you'll find arrowheads, spearheads, turn-of-the-century clothing, toys of yore, Victorian dollhouse furniture, and a model of the ship that took Herndon's life in 1857. The museum is open only periodically, usually one Saturday a month and on special occasions. You can call (703) 437-5556 to arrange a special tour through the Herndon Chamber of Commerce.

Leesburg

□ Federal Aviation Administration (FAA)

825 East Market Street. (703) 771-3522. Hour-long tours are given, for people eight years and older, Monday through Friday 9 A.M. to 3 P.M. (last tour starts at 2 P.M.); reservations are requested, but it's possible to be booked on a tour the day you call.

Included on the tour are examples of all the electronic equipment used to control the traffic flow caused by 1.3 million aircraft operations each year. You see what the controller does, watch the radarscopes, check the weather, and listen to air-to-ground communications. You learn what the FAA is, what different departments are involved, how quality assurance operates when there's been an accident, and how air-control specialists keep traffic moving safely in the skies.

McLean

□ Claude Moore Colonial Farm

6310 Georgetown Pike. (703) 442-7557. Open Wednesday through Sunday 10 A.M. to 4:30 P.M. April through December. Closed during inclement weather and on Thanksgiving and Christmas days. Adults, $2; children, $1. Membership available.

This small-scale farm is worked with the same tools and methods employed by farmers in the 18th century, in the days just prior to the Revolution. The busy family will answer your questions, as long as they don't relate to material after the 1770s. Among the animals present are bronzeback turkeys (they eat the green tobacco horn-worms that attack tobacco leaves), razorback and Ossabaw Island hogs, quarterhorses, cattle, bees, and Dung Hill Fowl chickens. A market is open for the market fairs held on the third full weekends of May, July, and September. Other seasonal celebrations are held on the third full weekends of June, August, and October.

Mount Vernon

☐ Mount Vernon Plantation

George Washington Memorial Parkway. (703) 780-2000. Open daily 9 A.M. to 5 P.M. March through October, until 4 P.M. the rest of the year. Adults, $6; senior citizens, $5; children 6 to 11, $3; free admission on national celebration of Washington's birthday, the third Monday in February. Self-guided tours, with guides available in the various rooms to talk about the room and answer questions; allow at least two hours to view the mansion, dependencies, and grounds. Tourmobile stop (summer only).

School students all over the country study George Washington and his Mount Vernon home, but seeing this grand estate and how the Washington family lived in the 1800s is completely different than reading about it all in a book. The mansion, which overlooks the mile-wide Potomac River, has been fastidiously restored with many original furnishings, including the bed on which Washington died.

Washington was a general and our first president, but he also was a surveyor (there are almost as many places in Virginia that boast "George Washington surveyed this property" as say "George Washington slept here") and a farmer. Some 3,000 acres of the estate's 8,000 acres were used for producing items for the home and for sale at such places as the old Alexandria Farmer's Market.

Therefore, in addition to the august-columned plantation house, there are about 18 dependencies, such as the coach house, greenhouse, smokehouse, stable, storehouse, spinning house, and slave quarters. Children particularly like the kitchen (it was too much of a fire risk to have the kitchen in the house) because they can see how food was prepared and served (no fast food or grocery stores in those days). There normally are no craft demonstrations, but visitors can see how laundry was done, how shoes were made, and the types of vehicles people traveled in.

Boy scouts, girl scouts, and campfire girls can walk along the historic trail and answer questions that will allow them to buy a Mount Vernon patch.

For four weeks after Washington's birthday, there are demonstrations of crafts of the colonial period and ceremonies at Washington's tomb and the Slave Memorial. These events are scheduled weekdays from 9:30 A.M. to 12:30 P.M.

Mount Vernon has one of the better gift shops, with the expected T-shirts and books about Washington, but also a nice selection of 18th-century games. On your visit to Mount Vernon you may also catch sight of an old tradition: All ships of the U.S. Navy and visiting navies offer a salute as they pass the estate.

Reston

☐ United States Geological Survey (USGS)

12201 Sunrise Valley Drive. (703) 648-4748. Tours are given Monday afternoon 1:30 to 4 P.M., Tuesday and Thursday 9:30 A.M. to 4 P.M.; reservations are requested. Depending on the age group, tours can be geared for anyone from prekindergartners on up, or you may be able to join a previously booked group. Information center is open Monday through Friday 8 A.M. to 4 P.M.

A wide range of geology-related activities occur here and the hour-long group tours can be tailored to specific interests. In general, scout and school groups see and learn about igneous and sedimentary rock formations, rock quarries, and dinosaurs.

Almost everything has a hands-on approach, from standing in the toe prints of a multimillion-year-old dinosaur to learning how to work a compass. You can even watch the presses printing some of the 1 million maps turned out here every year. Hikers, land planners, park service employees, the people involved in the decennial U.S. Census (the USGS maps the streets for the door-to-door surveys), and many others use USGS-produced maps, which range in scale from 1:24,000 to 1:250,000.

Outside, in the forest north of the building, is the Woodlands Walk, a marked trail with labeled trees. Guided or self-guided tours of the grounds are available, plus there's an orienteering program and a nature trail.

The Earth Science Information Center carries maps, books and pamphlets. The grounds are open daily for self-guided tours. A cafeteria is open for breakfast or lunch and picnic tables are located around the grounds.

Sterling

☐ Weather Bureau

Off Route 606. (703) 260-0107. Guided tours of 15 to 60 minutes are given Monday through Friday by appointment only (scout troops may make special arrangements for weekend tours); children below fourth grade will find the information too advanced. You can just walk in, but you take your chances on guide availability; severe weather will also affect tour possibilities.

A tour of this building, one of the newest and most modern weather offices in the country (occupied in March 1990) takes you into the operations area where three or four meteorologists issue forecasts for the mid-Atlantic states. (Yes, they operate on a 24-hour day.) They have a Doppler radar screen, which is more high-tech, detailed (they can see inside a storm), and colorful than older radar screens.

The first stop is the public desk, where the forecast you hear over the radio is formulated. A second area produces information for pilots and the FAA on the immediate geographic area and some more-distant points. Marine forecasting take place at the third desk, covering about 20 miles to the Chesapeake Bay and the coastal waters of Delaware, Maryland, and Virginia. There is also some offshore forecasting, reaching from central New Jersey to South Carolina and Bermuda. The fourth desk is a public-service operation that answers questions and takes reports from private contractors.

When you watch the radar map on your local weather channel, it comes from the weather bureau. The Sterling section provides the forecast for the Washington area cable channel carrying the weather.

Still another area of the bureau has hydrologists monitoring the rise and fall of major rivers to be able to warn residents and businesses, particularly along the riverbanks, of impending increases or decreases in water height.

Vienna

☐ Pet Farm Park

1228 Hunter Mill Road. (703) 759-3636 (general information recording), (703) 759-6761 (recording of weekend events). Open Monday through Friday 10 A.M. to 4 P.M., weekends 10 A.M. to 5 P.M. April through mid-November; extended weekday hours in summer. Adults, $5.50, children and senior citizens, $4.50; children under 2 free; add $1 in each category on weekends; season passes, $25.

Children have a chance to pet and feed cuddly baby animals, watch an egg hatch, whoop with a gibbon (that's not limited to children), ride a giant tortoise (50-pound weight limit) or a small African elephant named Sukara (300-pound limit), take a hayride or ride a pony, and see a buffalo, eland, elk and Watusi bull. They can look at the tiny South American squirrel monkeys on Monkey Island, but they can't pet them because the creatures bite. Because Fairfax County regulations prohibit keeping some adult animals, many of the little beasts here are babies that will be transferred to other operations. Cups of pet food are sold in the barn for 50 cents, so please do not bring food from home.

The farm regularly schedules special events, such as craft making, puppet shows, story hours, and animal shows. Once-a-year activities include sheep shearing and scarecrow making. Picnic tables and a playground are available.

☐ **Wolf Trap Farm Park for the Performing Arts**

Trap Road exit off Dulles Access Road. (703) 255-1900 (general information), (703) 255-1939 (BARNSTORM!), (703) 642-0862 (International Festival for Children). Open daily dawn to dusk.

This 100-acre park is the first and only national park in the country dedicated to the performing arts. There are no playgrounds, creeks, or other natural attractions, other than simply pretty grounds.

A full schedule of internationally renown artists, including rock stars, orchestras, jazz groups, and traveling Broadway shows, are presented just about every night during the summer. Seats in the open-air theater and lawn tickets are available. Shows are also given in the Barns, which makes productions possible during the winter.

A number of activities geared primarily to children are held from June to September. Among them are puppet shows in which live actors play the role of the characters, the Children's Theater in the Woods program, and a joyous, performance-filled, activity-intensive International Festival for Children every Labor Day weekend. The festival, which is directed toward children aged four to eight, features dancers, acrobats, face painting, singing, hula hoops, clowns, and crafts. This arts extravaganza finds 35,000 children and adults viewing performing artists from all over the world and participating in arts workshops. BARNSTORM! is a summer children's arts program given at 11 A.M. and 1 P.M. on the first Saturday of each month from October to May. Admission is $4, regardless of age. A free summer children's program is presented at 10 A.M. and 11 A.M. Monday through Friday, from June through August.

Hotels

Hotels in the Washington area can range from relatively inexpensive to very costly. Weekend rates generally are lower than midweek rates, although special events such as a presidential inauguration may place premium prices on every night or even initiate a minimum-stay requirement. Winter rates are less expensive than spring and summer rates. Hotels in the suburbs tend to be less expensive than downtown properties.

For a list of hotels and motels, check the American Automobile Association (AAA) tour guide or write to the tourism bureau(s) where you would like to stay. Look in the Before You Visit section of this book for addresses.

Some hotels provide special services and attractions for children. When evaluating a place, check for free or special accommodation rates and children's menus that not only offer smaller portions of an adult order, but items such as pizza and hamburgers that children like to eat. Also take note of whether a restaurant staff spots potentially fidgety children and provides a coloring book or other activity to keep them occupied while they are waiting for their food. Ask hotels about regularly planned activities, what they cost, the hours of operation, and if there is a mandatory reservation time (such as 3 P.M. the day of the service).

The following hotels have a children's program (such as Camp Hyatt), discounted or free lodging for children, a great view of the city, a children's menu, or an indoor pool (important when you're looking for something to do before or after a day of sightseeing and you don't feel like sitting in your room watching television). This is not a definitive list, but an alphabetical sampling of what's available. All of the hotels are located in Washington, unless otherwise indicated.

☐ Compri Hotel

2899 Jefferson Davis Highway, Crystal City, Arlington, Virginia. (800) 426-6774.

Children ages 12 and under stay free with their parents in the same room. A heated indoor pool, roaring fireplace, library with big-screen television, breakfast buffet, and evening peanut butter sandwiches are all included at the Compri.

☐ Hotel Washington

15th Street and Pennsylvania Avenue. (202) 638-5900. Old Town Trolley stop.

Children 14 and under stay free with parents in the same room at this centrally located hotel. The Sky Terrace restaurant offers a spectacular view during the summer, particularly in the evening. The terrace is open daily from 11:30 A.M. until 1 A.M., serving meals in the $5 to $15 price range and drinks. Arrive early, or start table hopping if you want the best front-row view. Lines form during the evening hours, but move rather quickly.

☐ Hyatt Hotels

Three in downtown Washington, Bethesda, Crystal City, Dulles, Reston, Arlington, Fair Lakes.

The nine Hyatt hotels in the Washington area all offer some form of the Camp Hyatt program, which provides board games, videos, books, and arts and crafts for children from age 3 to 15. Each hotel program has different hours, charges, and days of operation. These activity-oriented babysitting programs generally are open from 5 or 6 P.M. to 10 or 11 P.M. on Friday, Saturday, and sometimes Sunday evenings; they cost $4 to $5 per hour each for the first and sometimes second child, with lower prices for the third or more children.

Hyatt meals include a children's breakfast in the very affordable range of under $3 and lunch and dinner for under $5. At all Hyatts the second room is half the cost of the first room, so children can stay in a separate room, subject to availability.

Seven Hyatts have swimming pools, six of them indoors (Grand Hyatt Washington, Hyatt Regency Washington on Capitol Hill, Park Hyatt Hotel, Hyatt Regency Bethesda, Hyatt Regency Reston at Town Center, Hyatt Fair Lakes) and one outdoors (Hyatt Regency Crystal City). The Reston Hyatt also has an ice-skating rink and skate rentals. The Hyatt Regency and the Grand Hyatt are Old Town Trolley stops.

☐ Key Bridge Marriott

1401 Lee Highway, Arlington, Virginia. (703) 524-6400.

On the banks of the Potomac River, this Marriott houses the View Restaurant, a terrific spot from which to look out on the city at night-time and on Sunday at brunch. Brunch prices are adults, $23.95; children 14 to 20, $18.95; children 6 to 13, $14.95; and children 5 and under free. All children under 18 stay free with their parents in the same room.

☐ Loews L'Enfant Plaza

480 L'Enfant Plaza, SW. (202) 484-1000. Old Town Trolley stop.

Located on top of the L'Enfant Plaza subway station, an amusement arcade, and a shopping mall, the Loews features special getaway weekends with many benefits included in a stay. Children under 14 stay free with parents in the same room. There is an outdoor pool and a pretty good view of the city. Book ahead if you'd like to watch the Fourth of July fireworks from the 14th floor of the hotel.

☐ New Hampshire Suites

1121 New Hampshire Avenue, NW. (202) 457-0565, (800) 762-3777. Foggy Bottom subway station.

Suites come with kitchenettes, complete with coffee maker (complimentary coffee), mini-refrigerator (stocked with popcorn and pizza; charge), microwave oven, fresh flowers, and a note on the next day's weather forecast at nightly turndown. Children under 12 stay free with parents in the same suite. Free breakfast in the club room.

☐ Ramada Renaissance Techworld

999 Ninth Street, NW. (202) 898-9000.

Here you will find an indoor pool (children under 18 must be accompanied by an adult) and an active conservation program. The children's menu is on recycled paper and suggests several ways children can become involved in saving the earth and endangered species.

☐ Ritz-Carlton

2100 Massachusetts Avenue, NW. (202) 293-2100.

There is no charge for children under 12 staying with their parents in the same room. Every child who checks in receives a special children's amenity package, a fanny pack filled with healthful goodies such as raisins, fresh fruit, granola bars, and a nonedible Metrorail pass.

The hotel's Jockey Club restaurant, (202) 659-8001, the place for well-placed people to see and be seen, is aware that important adults have important children who like hamburgers and other unimportant food. More mature palates should try the superb crab cakes.

☐ Sheraton Carlton

16th and K streets, NW. (202) 638-2626, (800) 325-3535.

Children up to age 17 stay for free in their parents' room. A program for children up to 12 includes unlimited use of a selection of such electronic and game toys as Nintendo and checkers. Milk and cookies for the children arrive with evening turndown. Cribs for infants come with a complimentary basket of disposable diapers and a gift of a soft and fuzzy stuffed animal.

□ Washington Court Hotel

525 New Jersey Avenue, NW. (202) 628-2100.

In Mel Krupin's Signature Room (Krupin is a venerated Washington restaurateur), children are offered a special menu that might include a brontosaurus burger, or Fog Horn Leg Horn's world famous lower Alabama free-range fried chicken. Crayons are tableside.

□ Washington Hilton and Towers

1919 Connecticut Avenue at Columbia Road and T Street, NW. (202) 483-3000. Old Town Trolley stop.

Children of any age, including adults, stay free with their parents in the same room. There are three lighted tennis courts (charge) and a heated outdoor pool that's open 7 A.M. to 11 P.M. from late April to late October. The coffee shop has a children's menu and coloring books and crayons.

On the hotel's terrace level is an olivewood carving, *Monuments*, by Carl Malouf. It features some of Washington's most noteworthy architecture, places you may visit while in the area. If the area is not in use, stop by the sculpture to see if your children recognize the Washington Monument, the Supreme Court of the United States, the Old Post Office Building, and the Library of Congress.

□ Willard Inter-Continental

1401 Pennsylvania Avenue, NW. (202) 628-9100.

Children under 14 stay free with parents in the same room; over that age there is an additional $25 charge. Check the lobby ceiling for seals of the states. Children's items appear on the menu in Cafe Espresso and on the room-service menu. Holidays are a little more special, with cookies in the room and chocolate Santa Clauses.

Things to Do from A to Z

Activities listed here are located in Washington, D.C., unless otherwise noted.

Airplanes

Maryland

☐ **Paul E. Garber Facility**

1000 Old Silver Hill Road, Suitland. (202) 357-1400.

☐ **National Aeronautics and Space Administration (NASA)/
Goddard Space Flight Center, Visitor Center and Museum**

Soil Conservation Road, Greenbelt. (301) 286-8981.

Virginia

☐ **The Flying Circus**

1930s Barnstorming Airshow, Route 17, Bealeton. (703) 439-8661.

Washington

☐ **The National Air and Space Museum**

*Independence Avenue between Fourth and Seventh streets. (202) 357-2700,
(202) 357-1686 (recording about Langley theater presentations).*

Aquariums

Maryland

☐ **National Aquarium**

Pier 3, 501 East Pratt Street, Baltimore. (301) 576-3810.

Washington

☐ **National Aquarium**

*Department of Commerce, 14th Street and Constitution Avenue.
(202) 377-2825.*

Band Concerts (see also Tattoos)

During the summer, military, jazz, country, and big bands offer free outdoor concerts seven nights a week from Memorial Day through Labor Day, beginning at 8 P.M. Listen to local radio stations for cancellations due to weather.

Questions on band schedules may be answered by calling the following numbers: U.S. Navy Band (202) 433-6090, (703) 524-0830, (800) 821-8892; U.S. Army Band (202) 696-3647; U.S. Marine Corps Band (202) 694-3502; U.S. Air Force Band (202) 767-4310; or for general information on bands call (202) 475-1281.

Monday: U.S. Navy Band, U.S. Capitol, west side.

Tuesday: U.S. Army Band, Sylvan Theater on the Washington Monument grounds. U.S. Air Force Band, U.S. Capitol, west side.

Wednesday: U.S. Marine Corps Band, U.S. Capitol, west side. Big Band Concerts, Sylvan Theater on the Washington Monument grounds, (202) 619-7222 or (202) 619-PARK. U.S. Navy Band, Washington Navy Yard, 9 P.M., (202) 433-2218, (202) 433-2678 for reservations.

Thursday: U.S. Navy Band, U.S. Navy Memorial on Pennsylvania Avenue, (202) 347-6327.

Friday: U.S. Army Band, U.S. Capitol, west side. U.S. Air Force Band, Sylvan Theater on the Washington Monument grounds.

Saturday: Alternating military bands at the U.S. Navy Memorial on Pennsylvania Avenue.

Sunday: U.S. Marine Corps Band, Sylvan Theater on the Washington Monument grounds. Alternate Sundays: Concerts on the Canal Foundry Mall, 30th and Thomas Jefferson Streets, 1:30 to 4 P.M., (202) 619-7222.

Barge Rides

Maryland

☐ **C & O Canal Barge Rides**

11710 MacArthur Boulevard, Potomac. (301) 299-2026.

Washington

☐ **C & O Canal Barge Rides**

Foundry Mall, 1055 Thomas Jefferson Street (ticket office), Georgetown. (202) 472-4376 (recording), (202) 653-5844.

Battlefields

☐   **Antietam National Battlefield**
Maryland Route 65, 5831 Dunker Church Road, Sharpsburg, Maryland.
(301) 432-5124.

Bike Rentals

You may rent bikes at the following locations:

Washington

☐   **Fletchers' Boat House**
4940 Canal Road, NW. (202) 244-0461.

☐   **Metropolis Bicycles**
709 Eighth Street, SE. (202) 543-8900.

☐   **National Sculpture Garden Rink**
Ninth Street and Constitution Avenue, NW. (202) 737-6938,
(202) 347-9041.

☐   **Thompson's Boat Center**
Rock Creek Parkway and Virginia Avenue, NW. (202) 333-4861.

Virginia

☐   **The Bicycle Exchange**
1506C Belle View Boulevard, Alexandria. (703) 768-3444.

Biking

There are numerous gorgeous biking trails around the Washington area, providing shade and refreshing alternatives to Washington's summer heat and humidity. Some of them, however, can be very secluded and although you may be biking through the woods, this is a "big" city with all its potential dangers. Do not bike alone. Take identification with you, including your local hotel name and number if you're from out of town.

With that caveat out of the way, the trails will take you around lakes, up the C & O Canal, along the Potomac, through Rock Creek Park, and elsewhere. There are several publications for free or purchase at local bookstores and parks departments. Check with the appropriate tourism bureau for additional information. You may take your bike aboard the subway on weekends and all holidays except the Fourth of July, and on weekdays after 7 P.M. You need a pass, which costs $15 for five years, and you must attend a 30-minute class and take a simple test on the rules of use. Call (202) 962-1116 for specific information.

Boat Rentals

You can cool off on a hot Washington summer afternoon by renting everything from a canoe to a pedal boat (with required life jackets unless otherwise noted). The most famous crafts are the pedal boats (aka paddle boats) at the Tidal Basin, but there are other suburban locations. Generally, the boating season runs from late spring to early fall.

Maryland

☐ **Allen Pond**

3330 Northview Drive, Bowie. (301) 262-6200. Canoes, $2 per half hour; row boats, $3 per hour; paddle boats, $2.50 per half hour. Group rates available. Additional charge for nonresidents.

☐ **Clopper Lake**

Seneca State Park, 11950 Clopper Road, Gaithersburg. (301) 963-8788. Rowboats, $3 per hour; canoes and two-person pedal boats, $4 per hour; four-person pedal boats, $6 per hour. A one-hour pontoon-boat nature tour of the lake is 75 cents and operates Saturday and Sunday at 1:30, 3, 4:30, and 7:45 P.M. Reservations required for Saturday evening. Park admission is $4 for Maryland residents, $5 for out-of-state residents.

☐ **Cosca Lake**

Cosca Regional Park, 11000 Thrift Road, Clinton, (301) 868-2397. Rowboats and canoes, $2.50 per half hour, pedal boats, $3 per half hour.

☐ **Lake Needwood**

Rock Creek Regional Park, 15700 Needwood Lake Circle, Rockville. (301) 948-5053. Rowboats and canoes, $3.68 per hour, pedal boats, $3.94 per half hour.

☐ **Patuxent River**

Patuxent River Park, 16000 Croom Airport Road, Upper Marlboro. (301) 627-6074. Canoes, $10 per day. Reservations required.

☐ **Swains Lock**

Great Falls. (301) 299-9006. Canoes and rowboats, $6.65 per hour, $15.45 per day.

Virginia

☐ **Burke Lake Park**

7315 Ox Road, Fairfax Station. (703) 323-6600. Rowboats $9 per day, plus $1 for life jacket; $4.50 after 4 P.M.

☐ **Lake Fairfax**

1400 Lake Fairfax Drive, Reston. (703) 471-5414. Paddle boats, $3.50 per half hour.

☐ **Lake Fountainhead**

Fountainhead Regional Park, 10875 Hampton Road, Fairfax Station. (703) 250-9124. Flat-bottom rowboats, $9 per day, plus $1 for life jacket. You can bring your own electric motor, up to 10 horsepower.

Washington

☐ **Fletcher's Boat House**

Canal and Reservoir Roads, NW. (202) 244-0461. Canoes and rowboats, $13 weekdays, $14 weekends.

☐ **Jack's Boats**

3500 K Street. (202) 337-9642. Rowboats and canoes, $15 per day, $10 for two hours or less.

☐ **Thompson's Boat Center**

Rock Creek Parkway and Virginia Avenue, NW. (202) 333-4861. Rowboats and canoes, $4.75 per hour, $15 per day. Shells, $10 per hour; double shells, $15 per hour. Sunfish, $10 per hour.

☐ **Tidal Basin**

15th Street and Maine Avenue, SW. (202) 484-0206. Pedal boats (for two), $5.15 per hour.

Bookstores

Half a dozen children's bookstores are located in the Virginia and Washington area. In addition to having your child's favorite books, they have craft workshops, performances, chalk talks for aspiring authors and autograph collectors, and reading and storytelling sessions. At A Likely Storey, local politicians and administrators have been known to read their favorite stories. Cheshire Cat had a window display of monarch butterflies so observers could watch from egg to caterpillar to chrysalis. The Berenstain Bears Brother and Sister Bear characters have visited the Story Book Palace. And Clifford the Red Dog has been to the Book Nook.

Maryland

☐ **Audubon Book Shop**

8940 Jones Mill Road, Chevy Chase. (301) 652-3606.

Stores dealing with the natural sciences are also a favorite with children. The Maryland branch of the Audubon Book Shop is particularly good because it's on the grounds of the society's nature preserve, so you can combine a shopping trip with an exploration trip along the nature trail that winds through the spacious grounds.

☐ **Travelbooks Unlimited**

4931 Cordell Avenue, Bethesda. (301) 951-8533.

Virginia

☐ **A Likely Storey**

1555 King Street, Alexandria. (703) 836-2498.

☐ **Book Hook**

10312 Main Street, Fairfax. (703) 591-6545.

☐ **Imagination Station**

4530 Lee Highway, Arlington. (703) 522-2047.

☐ **Storybook Palace**

9538 Old Keene Road, Burke. (703) 644-2300.

Washington

☐ **A Happy Thought**

4836 MacArthur Boulevard. (202) 337-8300.

☐ **Audubon Book Shop**

1620 Wisconsin Avenue, NW, Georgetown. (202) 337-6062.

☐ **Cheshire Cat**

5121 Connecticut Avenue. (202) 244-3956.

☐ **National Zoo Book Store**

Education Building, 3000 Connecticut Avenue, NW. (202) 673-4967.

Brass Rubbing

Washington

☐ **London Brass Rubbing Centre**

4954 MacArthur Boulevard, Washington, D.C. (301) 279-7046.

Carousels

Maryland

☐ **Baltimore Zoo**

Druid Hill Park, off exit 7 of Interstate 83. (301) 366-5466.

☐ **Columbia Mall**

10300 Little Patuxent Parkway, Columbia. (301) 730-3300.

☐ **Glen Echo Park**

MacArthur Boulevard at Goldsboro Road, Glen Echo. (301) 492-6663.

☐ **Watkins Regional Park**

Enterprise Road, Largo. (301) 249-9220.

☐ **Wheaton Regional Park**

2000 Shorefield Road, Wheaton. (301) 622-0056.

Virginia

☐ **Burke Lake Park**

7315 Ox Road, Fairfax Station. (703) 323-6600.

☐ **Lake Accotink Park**

5660 Heming Avenue, Springfield. (703) 569-3464.

☐ **Lake Fairfax**

1400 Lake Fairfax Drive, Reston. (703) 471-5415.

☐ **Lee District Park**

6601 Telegraph Road, Alexandria. (703) 922-9841.

Washington

On the Mall

Constitution Avenue and Tenth Street.

Cemeteries

Virginia

☐ **Arlington National Cemetery**

Off Memorial Drive, Arlington. (703) 692-0931.

Washington

☐ **Congressional Cemetery**

18th and E streets. (202) 543-0539.

Churches

☐ **Franciscan Monastery**

1400 Quincy Street. (202) 526-6800.

☐ **National Shrine of the Immaculate Conception**

Michigan Avenue and Fourth Street. (202) 526-8300.

☐ **Washington National Cathedral**

Massachusetts and Wisconsin avenues, at Woodley Road. (202) 364-6616 (recording), (202) 537-6200.

Computers

☐ **Tech 2000**

Techworld Plaza, 800 K Street. (202) 842-0500.

Drill Teams (See Band Concerts, Tattoos)

Equestrian Centers

☐ **Prince George's Equestrian Center**
Upper Marlboro, Maryland. (301) 952-4740.

Farms

Maryland

☐ **Carroll County Farm Museum**
Westminster. (301) 848-7775.

☐ **Hardbargain Farm**
Alice Ferguson Foundation, Accokeek. (301) 283-2695.

☐ **National Colonial Farm**
3400 Bryan Point Road, Accokeek. (301) 283-2113.

☐ **Old MacDonald's Farm**
Wheaton Regional Park, 2000 Shorefield Road, Wheaton. (301) 384-9447.

☐ **Oxon Hill Children's Farm**
6411 Oxon Hill Road, Oxon Hill. (301) 839-1177.

Virginia

☐ **Claude Moore Colonial Farm**
6310 Georgetown Pike, McLean. (703) 442-7557.

☐ **Pet Farm Park**
1228 Hunter Mill Road, Vienna. (703) 759-3636, 759-6761 (recording of weekends events).

Turkey Run Farm
McLean. (703) 557-1357.

Fish Market

☐ **Maine Avenue Fish Market**
Maine Avenue and Eighth Street.

Forts

Maryland

☐ **Fort McHenry National Monument and Historic Shrine**
East Fort Avenue, Baltimore. (301) 962-4290.

☐ **Fort Washington**
Fort Washington Road, Fort Washington. (301) 763-4600.

Virginia

☐ **Fort Ward Museum and Park**
4301 West Braddock Road, Alexandria. (703) 833-4848.

Frisbee Golf

Maryland

☐ **Calvert Road Community Park**
5202 Old Calvert Road, College Park.

☐ **Seneca Creek State Park**
11950 Clopper Road, Gaithersburg. (301) 963-8788.

Virginia

☐ **Bluemont Park**
North Manchester Street and Wilson Boulevard, Arlington. (703) 554-8643.

☐ **Bull Run Regional Park**
7700 Bull Run Drive, Centreville. (703) 631-0550.

☐ **Burke Lake Park**
7315 Ox Road, Fairfax Station. (703) 323-6601.

☐ **McLean Central Park**
1468 Dolley Madison Boulevard, McLean.

☐ **Pohick Bay Regional Park**
10651 Gunston Road, Lorton. (703) 339-6104.

Galleries

Maryland

☐   **Walters Art Gallery**

600 North Charles Street, at Mount Vernon Square, Baltimore. (301) 547-ARTS (recording), (301) 547-9000.

Virginia

☐   **Torpedo Factory**

105 North Union Street, Alexandria. (703) 838-4565, (703) 683-0693 (tours).

Washington

☐   **National Museum of American Art**

Eighth Street between F and G streets. (202) 357-2700.

☐   **Ansel Adams Collection**

900 17th Street, second floor. (202) 833-2300.

☐   **Art Barn Gallery**

Rock Creek Park, 2401 Tilden Street. (202) 244-2482.

☐   **Arthur M. Sackler Gallery**

1050 Independence Avenue. (202) 357-2700, (202) 357-2041, (202) 357-4886 (Education Department).

☐   **Corcoran Gallery of Art**

17th Street and New York Avenue. (202) 638-3211, (202) 638-1439.

☐   **Fondo del Sol Visual Arts Center**

2112 R Street. (202) 483-2777.

☐   **Freer Gallery of Art**

12th Street and Jefferson Drive. (202) 357-2700.

☐   **National Gallery of Art**

Sixth Street at Constitution Avenue. (202) 842-6358, (202) 737-4215.

☐   **National Portrait Gallery**

Eighth Street between F and G streets. (202) 357-2700.

☐ **Navy Combat Art Center**
Ninth and M streets, Building 67, (202) 433-3815.

☐ **Phillips Collection**
1600 21st Street. (202) 387-0961 (recording), (202) 387-2151.

☐ **Renwick Gallery**
17th Street and Pennsylvania Avenue. (202) 357-2700.

☐ **Washington Project for the Arts**
400 Seventh Street. (202) 347-8304.

Gardens

Maryland

☐ **Battle Creek Cypress Swamp Sanctuary**
Grays Road off Route 506, Prince Frederick. (301) 535-5327.

☐ **Brookside Gardens**
1500 Glenallen Avenue, Wheaton. (301) 949-8230 (recording).

☐ **McGrillis Gardens**
6910 Greentree Road, Bethesda. (301) 949-8230.

Washington

☐ **Chinese Gardens**
800 K Street.

☐ **Constitution Gardens**
*Between the Washington Monument and the Lincoln Memorial.
(202) 426-6841.*

☐ **Floral Library**
*Near the Tidal Basin, between the Washington Monument and Jefferson
Memorial. (202) 619-7222.*

☐ **Enid A. Haupt Garden**
Tenth Street and Independence Avenue. (202) 357-1926.

☐ **Kenilworth Aquatic Gardens**

1900 Anacostia Avenue at Douglas Street. (202) 426-6905.

☐ **Tudor Place**

1644 31st Street. (202) 965-0400.

☐ **United States Botanic Garden**

Maryland Avenue, near First Street. (202) 225-8333.

☐ **United States National Arboretum,**

3501 New York Avenue. (202) 475-4815.

Golf Courses

There are many public courses in the Greater Washington area. Here are three within Washington. Call for tee times and greens fees. Some do not accept charge cards.

☐ **East Potomac Golf Course**

East Potomac Park, SW. (202) 836-9007. One 18-hole course and two 9-hole courses.

☐ **Langston Golf Course**

26th Street and Benning Road, NE. (202) 397-8638. 18-hole course. Driving range.

☐ **Rock Creek Golf Course**

Rock Creek Park, 16th and Rittenhouse streets, NW. (202) 882-7332. 18-hole course. Pitching range.

Holograms

☐ **Holography World**

Techworld Plaza, 800 K Street. (202) 408-1833.

Horseback Riding

Horseback riding takes advantage of the many scenic wonders in the area. Additionally, several evening rides are offered for those who want something to do after the museums have closed. Most horses are tacked western, but some operations will tack them English, upon request.

Maryland

☐ **Breezy Hill Ranch**

16603 Crain Highway, Brandywine. (301) 372-6772. Unguided ride, $12 per hour; guided ride, $17 per hour.

☐ **Callithea Riding Stables of Potomac**

15000 River Road, Potomac. (301) 977-3839. Unguided ride, $20 per hour. Unlimited riding during the week and six hours maximum on weekends for seldom-scene views of the Potomac and surrounding areas. Minimum age is 16, but younger children may ride ponies with parents at lead.

☐ **Double S-S Stables**

16211 McKendree Road, Brandywine. (301) 372-8921. Unguided ride, $12 per hour on weekdays and $16 per hour on weekends and holidays. Ride through 80 acres of white-fenced fields and evergreen-edged paths.

☐ **Piscataway Stables**

10775 Piscataway Road, Clinton. (301) 297-7711. Weekdays, $10 per hour; weekends, $15 per hour; deposit required. Children are welcome but must prove their ability to ride.

☐ **Potomac Polo School**

Hughes and River roads, Poolesville (301) 972-7241. Two-hour guided ride, $30. Overnight rides through the Appalachian Mountains and other specialty rides. Reservations required.

☐ **Rock Bottom Farm Riding School**

21930 New Hampshire Avenue, Brookville. (301) 924-2612. Unguided ride, $18 per hour; guided ride, $20 per hour. Reserve horses at least two days in advance. You must prove your ability (including a low jump) and tack your horse before your ride and then untack it upon completion.

☐ **Wheaton Regional Park Stables**

1101 Glenallen Avenue, Wheaton. (301) 622-3311. Guided ride, $10 per hour; reservations required. English saddles.

Virginia

☐ **Equestrian Enterprises**

966 Millwood Road, Great Falls. (703) 759-2474. Guided ride, $16 per hour; minimum of two hours. Summertime moonlight rides and all-day safari rides. Hours by appointment; reservations required.

☐ **Marriott Ranches**

Route 1, Hume. (703) 364-2627. Ninety-minute guided ride, $20; two-hour guided ride, $30; four-hour guided ride, $40. Overnight rides available. Reservations required.

Washington

☐ **Rock Creek Park Horse Center**

Military and Glover roads, NW (202) 362-0118. Guided ride, $13 per hour. Reservations required during the week. Minimum age is 12.

Ice Skating

Maryland

☐ **Bowie Ice Arena**

Allen Pond, Bowie. (301) 249-2088.

☐ **Cabin John Regional Park**

10610 Westlake Drive, Potomac. (301) 365-0585 (recording).

☐ **Herbert W. Wells Ice Rink**

5211 Calvert Road, College Park. (301) 277-0654.

☐ **Tucker Road Ice Rink**

1771 Tucker Road, Oxon Hill. (301) 248-2508.

☐ **Wheaton Regional Park**

Orebaugh Avenue, Wheaton. (301) 649-2250.

Washington

☐ **C & O Canal**

Georgetown. Free; check with National Park Service first. (202) 485-9666.

☐ **National Sculpture Garden Rink**

Ninth Street and Constitution Avenue.

☐ **Pershing Park Rink**

14th Street and Pennsylvania Avenue. (202) 737-6938, (202) 347-9041.

☐ **Reflecting Pool**

Between the Washington Monument and Lincoln Memorial. Free; check with National Park Service first. (202) 485-9666.

Jousting

Jousting, the state sport of Maryland, can be seen on the grounds of the Washington Monument usually during October. (202) 426-6700 for scheduled tournaments.

Kite-Flying

Annual kite-flying competition held in late March or early April on the Washington Monument grounds. Write to Margo Brown, 6636 Kirkley Avenue, McLean, Virginia 22101, for information. Enclose a self-addressed, stamped envelope with two first-class stamps on it.

Library

☐ **Library of Congress**

10 First Street, SE (First and East Capitol streets). (202) 707-5000.

Magic Shops

Maryland

☐ **Barry's Magic Shop**

11234 Georgia Avenue, Wheaton. (301) 933-0373.

Washington

☐ **Al's Magic Shop**

1012 Vermont Avenue, NW. (202) 789-2800

Mill

☐ **Peirce Mill**

Rock Creek Park, Beach Drive and Tilden Street. (202) 426-6908.

Monuments and Memorials

Maryland

☐ **Fort McHenry National Monument and Historic Shrine**
East Fort Avenue, Baltimore. (301) 962-4290.

Virginia

☐ **Roosevelt Island**
George Washington Memorial Parkway, Great Falls. (703) 285-2598.

☐ **United States Marine Corps War Memorial (Iwo Jima)**
Adjacent to Arlington National Cemetery. (202) 433-6060.

Washington

☐ **Jefferson Memorial**
South bank of Tidal Basin, 14th Street and East Basin Drive, SW, East Potomac Park. (202) 426-6822.

☐ **Lincoln Memorial**
Memorial Circle between Constitution and Independence avenues. (202) 426-6841.

☐ **United States Navy Memorial Visitors Center**
Pennsylvania Avenue at Eighth Street. (800) 821-8892. (703) 524-0830.

☐ **Vietnam Veterans Memorial**
Constitution Avenue between Henry Balm Drive and 21st Street. (202) 485-9666.

☐ **Washington Monument**
The Mall between 15th and 17th streets. (202) 426-6839.

Museums (See also Galleries)

Maryland

☐ **Babe Ruth Birthplace**
Baltimore Orioles Museum, 216 Emory Street, Baltimore. (301) 727-1539.

☐ **Baltimore Museum of Art**

Art Museum Drive, Baltimore. (301) 396-7101, (301) 396-6320 (Education Office).

☐ **B & O Railroad Museum**

901 West Pratt Street, at Poppleton Street, Baltimore. (301) 752-2490 (information).

☐ **B & O Railroad Station Museum**

Maryland Avenue and Main Street, Ellicott City. (301) 461-1944.

☐ **Cloisters Children's Museum**

10440 Falls Road, Brooklandville. (301) 823-2550, (301) 823-2551 (schedules and tickets to special events).

☐ **National Aeronautics and Space Administration (NASA)/ Goddard Space Flight Center**

Visitor Center and Museum. Soil Conservation Road, Greenbelt. (301) 286-8981.

☐ **Rose Hill Manor: Children's Museum and Park**

1161 North Market Street, Frederick. (301) 694-1648, (301) 694-1646.

Washington

☐ **National Museum of African Art**

950 Independence Avenue. (202) 357-2700, (202) 357-4860 (Education Department).

☐ **National Air and Space Museum,**

Independence Avenue between Fourth and Seventh streets, (202) 357-2700, (202) 357-1686 (recording about Langley Theater presentations).

☐ **National Museum of American History**

14th Street between Constitution Avenue and Madison Drive. (202) 357-2700.

☐ **Anacostia Neighborhood Museum**

1901 Fort Place. (202) 287-3369.

☐ **Anderson House Museum**

2118 Massachusetts Avenue. (202) 785-2040.

☐   **Arts and Industries Building**

900 Jefferson Drive. (202) 357-2700, (202) 357-1500 (Discovery Theater reservations, voice or TDD).

☐   **Bethune Museum and Archives**

1318 Vermont Avenue. (202) 332-1233.

☐   **B'nai B'rith Klutznick Museum and Exhibit Hall**

1640 Rhode Island Avenue. (202) 393-5284, ext. 203.

☐   **Capital Children's Museum**

800 Third Street at H Street. (202) 543-8600.

☐   **Children's Museum of Washington**

4954 MacArthur Boulevard. (202) 337-4954.

☐   **Columbia Historical Society**

1307 New Hampshire Avenue. (202) 785-2068.

☐   **Daughters of the American Revolution (DAR) Museum**

1776 D Street. (202) 879-3239 (children's tour and children's program information).

☐   **Dumbarton Oaks**

1703 32nd Street. (202) 342-3200, (202) 342-3212.

☐   **Explorer's Hall**

National Geographic Society, 17th and M streets. (202) 857-7588.

☐   **Frederick Douglass National Historic Site**

1411 W Street. (202) 426-5960.

☐   **Hillwood**

4155 Linnean Avenue. (202) 686-5807.

☐   **Hirschhorn Museum and Sculpture Garden**

Eighth Street and Independence Avenue. (202) 357-2700.

☐   **Department of the Interior Museum**

18th and C streets. (202) 208-4743.

☐ **Lincoln Museum**

511 Tenth Street. (202) 426-6924.

☐ **Marine Corps Museum**

Building 58, Ninth and M streets. (202) 433-3534.

☐ **Meridian House International**

1624 and 1630 Crescent Place. (202) 667-6800.

☐ **Museum of Modern Art of Latin America**

201 18th Street. (202) 458-6019.

☐ **National Archives**

Constitution Avenue between Seventh and Ninth streets. (202) 501-5000 (recorded information about special program events).

☐ **National Building Museum**

Judiciary Square, F Street between Fourth and Fifth streets. (202) 272-2448.

☐ **Museum of Natural History**

Tenth Street between Constitution Avenue and Madison Drive. (202) 357-2700.

☐ **Navy Museum**

Ninth and M streets, (202) 433-2651.

☐ **Old Stone House**

3051 M Street. (202) 426-6851.

☐ **Petersen House**

526 Tenth Street. (202) 426-6830.

☐ **Textile Museum**

2320 S Street. (202) 667-0441.

☐ **Tudor Place**

1644 31st Street. (202) 965-0400.

☐ **The U.S.S. *Barry,***

Ninth and M streets. (202) 433-3377.

☐ **Washington Doll House and Toy Museum**

5236 44th Street. (202) 244-0024.

☐ **National Museum Women in the Arts**

1250 New York Avenue. (202) 783-5000.

☐ **Woodrow Wilson House**

2340 S Street. (202) 673-4034.

Nature Centers

Nature centers feature numerous family activities, generally geared to specific age groups. These events may be watching a lunar eclipse, canoeing, field trips to other centers, woodland walks, animal interviews, butterfly hunts, boat rides, beaver searches, amphibious adventures, seeing nocturnal animals, and countless more. Check the local papers for schedules, or call the nearest center for topics.

Maryland

☐ **Audubon Naturalist Society**

8940 Jones Mill Road, Chevy Chase. (301) 652-5964.

☐ **Black Hills Regional Park**

13440 West Old Baltimore Road, Boyds. (301) 972-9458.

☐ **Brookside Nature Center**

Wheaton Regional Park, 1400 Glenallen Avenue, Wheaton. (301) 946-9071.

☐ **Chesapeake Wildlife Sanctuary**

17308 Queen Anne Bridge Road, Bowie. (301) 390-7010.

☐ **Clearwater Nature Center**

1100 Thrift Road, Clinton. (301) 297-4575.

☐ **Hawk's Reach Nature Center**

Little Bennett Regional Park, 23701 Frederick Road, Clarkesburg. (301) 972-9458.

☐ **Lathrop E. Smith Environmental Education Center**

5110 Meadowside Lane, Rockville. (301) 924-4141.

☐ **Little Bennett**
23701 Frederick Road, Clarksburg. (301) 972-9458.

☐ **Locust Grove**
7777 Democracy Boulevard, Potomac. (301) 299-1990.

☐ **Maydale Nature Center**
1638 Maydale Drive, Silver Spring. (301) 384-9447.

☐ **Meadowside Nature Center**
5100 Meadowside Lane, Rockville. (301) 924-4141.

☐ **Merkle Wildlife Sanctuary Visitor Center**
Upper Marlboro. (301) 888-1410.

☐ **Oregon Ridge Nature Center**
13555 Beaver Dam Road, Cockeysville. (301) 887-1815.

☐ **Piney Run Park**
30 Martz Road, Sykesville. (301) 795-3274.

☐ **30th Street Nature Center**
4210 30th Street, Mount Rainier. (301) 927-2163.

☐ **Watkins Park Nature Center**
301 Watkins Park Drive, Upper Marlboro. (301) 249-6202.

Virginia

☐ **Hidden Oaks Nature Center**
Annandale Community Park, 4020 Hummer Road, Annandale. (703) 941-1065.

☐ **Ramsey Nature Center**
5700 Sanger Avenue, West Alexandria. (703) 838-4839.

☐ **Riverbend Park and Nature Center**
8814 Jeffrey Road, Great Falls. (703) 759-3211.

Washington

☐ **Rock Creek Nature Center**
5200 Glover Road. (202) 426-6828.

Observatories

Maryland

☐ **University of Maryland Observatory**
Metzerott Road at University Boulevard, College Park. (301) 454-3001.

Washington

☐ **United States Naval Observatory**
Massachusetts Avenue at 34th Street. (202) 653-1543.

Parks (See also Regional Parks)

Maryland

☐ **Glen Echo Park**
7300 MacArthur Boulevard, Glen Echo. (301) 492-6282.

☐ **Great Falls Park**
Off MacArthur Boulevard, Potomac.

☐ **Rose Hill Manor: Children's Museum and Park**
1161 North Market Street. (301) 694-1648, (301) 694-1646.

Virginia

☐ **Great Falls National Park**
9200 Old Dominion Drive, Great Falls. (703) 285-2966.

Washington

☐ **Anacostia Park**
1900 Anacostia Drive. (202) 433-1152.

☐ **Hains Point, or East Potomac Park**
Peninsula between the Washington Channel and the Potomac River.

☐ **Lincoln Park**
East Capitol Street, between 11th and 13th streets.

☐ **Rock Creek Park**
Tilden Street and Beach Drive. (202) 426-6832.

Playground (Unusual)

☐ **Abingdon Elementary School**

3035 South Abingdon Street, behind Abingdon School, Arlington, Virginia. (703) 845-7664. Features an unusual playground in the shape of the United States. An alligator is Florida; the high climbers are the Rockies.

Planetariums

Maryland

☐ **Davis Planetarium, Maryland Science Center**

601 Light Street, Baltimore. (301) 685-5225 (recording), 685-2370 (office).

Washington

☐ **Albert Einstein Planetarium, National Air and Space Museum**

Independence Avenue between Fourth and Seventh streets. (202) 357-2700.

☐ **Rock Creek Nature Center**

5200 Glover Road. (202) 426-6828

Polo

Maryland

☐ **Potomac Polo Club**

10250 River Road, Potomac. (301) 881-5040. Sunday at 4 P.M. General admission, $5; reserved seats, $8; parking, $7 per car.

Washington

☐ **West Potomac Park**

Near the Lincoln Memorial. (202) 485-9666. Sunday at 2 P.M.

Post Office Tours

☐ **United States Post Office**

900 Brentwood Road. (202) 636-1208.

Regional Parks (See also Parks)

Maryland

☐ **Black Hill Regional Park**
13440 West Old Baltimore Road, Boyds. (301) 972-9397.

☐ **Cabin John Regional Park**
7400 Tuckerman Lane, Rockville. (301) 299-4555.

☐ **Fairland Regional Park**
14110 Old Gunpowder Road, Laurel. (301) 953-0294.

☐ **Little Bennett Regional Park**
23701 Frederick Road, Clarksburg. (301) 972-6581.

☐ **Louise Cosca Regional Park**
Thrift Road, Clinton. (301) 858-1397.

☐ **Patuxent River Park**
Box 3380, Upper Marlboro. (301) 629-6074.

☐ **Rock Creek Regional Park**
6700 Needlewood Road, Rockville. (301) 948-5053.

☐ **Watkins Regional Park**
301 Watkins Park Drive, Upper Marlboro. (301) 249-6900.

☐ **Wheaton Regional Park**
2000 Shorefield Road, Wheaton. (301) 622-0056.

Virginia

☐ **Washington and Old Dominion Railroad Regional Park**
5400 Ox Road, Fairfax Station (park office address). (703) 352-5900, (703) 437-1910 (trail office).

Road Rallies

Road rallying is a popular activity in the Washington, D.C. area and during nice weather you can find a rally almost every Sunday. For coordination purposes, call or write the Washington Rally Club, 7705 Beach Tree Road, Bethesda, Maryland 20817. (202) 822-2876.

Science Center

☐ **Maryland Science Center**
601 Light Street, Baltimore. (301) 685-5225 (recording), 685-2370 (office), 837-IMAX (IMAX information).

Ships

Maryland

☐ **U.S. Frigate** *Constellation*
Pier 1, Pratt Street, Baltimore. (301) 539-1797.

Washington

☐ **U.S.S.** *Barry*
Ninth and M streets. (202) 433-3377.

Shooting

☐ **Prince George's Public Shooting Center**
10400 Good Luck Road, Glen Dale, Maryland. (301) 577-1477.

Skiing

You'll find moderately good ski slopes in western Maryland, Virginia, and Pennsylvania, all within 155 miles of Washington. Ski Liberty is only 65 miles away, so you can finish a meeting or a day's sightseeing, hop in your car, ski for a couple of hours, and return for the next day's meeting or sightseeing. Most ski areas have night skiing and snow-making machines. Ski season generally is late November through March and ski areas usually run out of skiers before they run out of snow. That means you can practically have the slopes to yourself in March. Local radio stations give weekend snow-condition reports, or call the numbers listed. The slopes listed are within 155 miles, or about a three-hour drive.

Pennsylvania

☐ **Blue Knob**
Claysburg. (814) 239-5111. 150 miles. Snow report (800) 458-3403.

☐ **Doe Mountain**

Macungie. (215) 682-7109. 155 miles. Snow report (215) 682-7107.

☐ **Ski Liberty**

Fairfield. (717) 642-8282. 65 miles. Snow report (800) 827-4766.

Virginia

☐ **Bryce Mountain**

Basye. (703) 856-2121. 120 miles. Snow report (703) 856-2151.

☐ **Wintergreen**

Wintergreen. (804) 325-2200, (800) 325-2200. 145 miles. Snow report (804) 325-7669. Active children's program including instruction, child care and Kids Night Out for children 4 to 12 while parents enjoy a night of skiing.

Skiing (Indoors)

☐ **Aspen Hill Ski Training Center**

14501 Bel Pre Road, Silver Spring, Maryland. (301) 598-5200.

Sports Arena

☐ **Capital Center**

1 Harry S Truman Drive, Landover, Maryland. (301) 350-3400. Also used for concerts.

Swimming Pools

There are a number of indoor pools in the area, in addition to hotel pools listed in the Hotels section.

Maryland

☐ **Allentown Road Fitness Center**

7210 Allentown Road, Fort Washington. (301) 449-5566.

☐ **Ellen E. Linson**

5211 Calvert Road, College Park. (301) 277-0654.

☐ **Robert I. Bickford Natatorium**

Prince George's Community College, Landover Road, Largo. (Indoor, 50 meter pool). (301) 322-0504.

☐   **Theresa Banks Memorial Pool**

8615 McLain Avenue, Glenarden. (301) 772-5515.

Virginia

☐   **Herndon Community Center**

814 Ferndale Avenue, Herndon. (703) 787-7300.

Washington

☐   **Capitol East Natatorium**

635 North Carolina Avenue, SE. (202) 724-4495

Tattoos (See also Band Concerts)

During the summer the U.S. Army and the U.S. Marine Corps offer a series of exciting tattoos. These demonstrations of precision marching, rifle tossing, and silent drills that involve circling and crisscrossing through an ornate maze of half steps and spinning rifles, are, to choose a child's word, awesome.

Tuesday: U.S. Marine Drum and Bugle Corps and Silent Drill Platoon, Iwo Jima Memorial, 7:30 P.M. (202) 485-9666.

Wednesday: Third U.S. Infantry and the U.S. Army Band, Ellipse grounds, 7 P.M. (202) 696-3647.

Wednesday: Torchlight Tattoo, Jefferson Memorial, June through August, 8 P.M.

Friday: Marine Barracks, Eighth and I streets, May through August, 8:45 P.M. (202) 433-6060.

Tennis

☐   **Cosca Tennis Bubble**

11000 Thrift Road, Clinton, Maryland. (301) 868-6462.

☐   **Watkins Regional Park**

301 Watkins Park Drive, Upper Marlboro, Maryland. (301) 249-9325.

Theaters

Virginia

☐   **Wolf Trap Farm Park for the Performing Arts**

Trap Road exit off Dulles Access Road, Virginia. (703) 255-1900 (general information), (703) 255-1939 (BARNSTORM!), (703) 642-0862 (International Festival for Children).

Washington

☐ **Arena Stage**

Sixth Street and Maine Avenue. (202) 488-3300 (box office).

☐ **Constitution Hall**

1776 D Street. (202) 638-2661.

☐ **Ford's Theatre**

511 Tenth Street. (202) 638-2941.

☐ **John F. Kennedy Center for the Performing Arts**

New Hampshire Avenue at Rock Creek Parkway. (202) 467-4600, (800) 444-1324 (recording about shows and ticket purchase), (202) 416-8341 (tours).

☐ **National Theatre**

1321 Pennsylvania Avenue. (202) 628-6161 (ticket information), (202) 783-3372 (schedule for Saturday morning and Monday night children's programs).

Theme Parks

There are six theme parks within a three-hour drive of Washington. They are all open daily during the summer, and most are open weekends during April, May, September, and October. Admissions run about $21 for everyone over three (Wild World is about $15), with discounts for senior citizens, off-season attendance, or late-evening and next-day packages.

Maryland

☐ **Wild World**

P.O. Box 1610, Mitchellville. (301) 249-1500.

New Jersey

☐ **Six Flags Great Adventure**

Jackson. (201) 928-2000.

Pennsylvania

☐ **Hersheypark**

100 West Hersheypark Drive, Hershey. (800) HER-SHEY.

☐ **Sesame Place**

Langhorne. (215) 757-1100.

Virginia

☐ **Busch Gardens**

The Old Country, P.O. Box Drawer F-C, Williamsburg. (804) 253-3350, (800) 832-5665.

☐ **Kings Dominion**

P.O. Box 166, Doswell. (800) 876-5000.

Trains and Trolleys

☐ **B & O Railroad Museum**

901 West Pratt Street, at Poppleton Street, Baltimore, Maryland. (301) 752-2490.

☐ **B & O Railroad Station Museum**

Maryland Avenue and Main Street, Ellicott City, Maryland. (301) 461-1944.

☐ **National Capital Trolley Museum**

Bonifant Road between Layhill Road and New Hampshire Avenue, Wheaton, Maryland. (301) 384-6088.

Transportation

☐ **Metropolitan Area Transit Authority (WMATA)**

600 Fifth Street, NW. (202) 637-7000.

☐ **Old Town Trolley Tours**

(202) 269-3020 (recording), (202) 269-3021.

☐ **Tourmobile**

(202) 554-7950 (recording), (202) 554-7020 (information).

Walking Tours

A number of walking tours are offered through various tour services by calling First Class, an alternative, noncredit adult-education organization, (202) 797-5102. Among the tours available are Capitol Hill, Inside the Capitol, Walking Tour of Arlington Cemetery, Adams-Morgan Walking Tour, and Monumental Washington.

Windsurfing

Several places in the area offer windsurfing lessons, but this list will concentrate on rentals. Other opportunities can be found in Maryland at Ocean City and Annapolis.

☐ **Belle Haven Marina**

George Washington Memorial Parkway, Alexandria, Virginia. (703) 768-0018. Weekdays, $9 per hour; weekends, $10 per hour.

☐ **Washington Sailing Marina**

George Washington Memorial Parkway, Alexandria, Virginia. (703) 548-9027. First hour, $11; $9 each additional hour, plus a $20 checkout fee if you are uncertified or haven't sailed there before.

Zoos

Maryland

☐ **Baltimore Zoo**

Druid Hill Park off exit 7 of Interstate 83, Baltimore. (301) 366-5466 (recording), 396-7102 (administration).

☐ **Catoctin Mountain Zoological Park**

U.S. 15, Thurmont. (301) 271-7488. (301) 662-2579.

☐ **Noah's Ark**

Cabin John Regional Park, Tuckerman Lane, Bethesda. (301) 299-4555.

Washington

☐ **National Zoological Park**

3000 block of Connecticut Avenue. (202) 357-2700 (Smithsonian information), (202) 673-4717 (direct line to zoo), (202) 357-1729 (TDD), (202) 357-1697 (voice recording).

Index

This book and the others in the Places to Go… series are available at your local bookstore. For a color catalog of all our books call or write:

Chronicle Books
275 Fifth Street
San Francisco, CA 94103
1-800-722-6657